A FUTURE

AND A HOPE

THE STORY OF

RAYS OF HOPE MINISTRIES

MUMBAI - INDIA

By Petra van der Zande

ISBN 978 965 7542 07 1

Summary:
The story of Rays of HOPE Ministries in Mumbai, India who work amongst the orphans, HIV and AIDS carriers, widows, and prostitutes. A chronicle of true servant-hood, God's guidance, provision and miracles. A modern-day, Indian version of George Müller of Bristol.

Printed in Jerusalem, Israel, by PRINTIV

**Copies can be ordered through
www.lulu.com**

**or by writing to email:
tsurtsinapublications@gmail.com**

"I am a Father to the fatherless. I am sending you as my ambassador of love to these little ones whom the world has forgotten."
Mahesh Chavda, *Only Love can do a Miracle*

THIS BOOK IS DEDICATED TO
THE NEEDY CHILDREN
AROUND THE WORLD

THE

ORPHANS

HIV-POSTIVE

BONDED SLAVES

STREET CHILDREN

THE ONES WHO WERE SOLD

INTO PROSTITUTION

AND CHILDREN OF PROSTITUTES

MAY THE GOD OF MERCY
FULFILL THEIR LONGING
FOR A FUTURE AND A HOPE

CONTENTS

CONTENTS

CONTENTS

FOREWORD

By Dr. Al Nucciarone

One day, while my wife and I were driving, we received a life changing telephone call. On the line was Pastor Manoj Magar of Rays of HOPE Ministries in India. He had received an email from our daughter, Allison, who inquired about the possibility of a short-term ministry trip to work with his orphanage. Manoj was so excited that I was the pastor of Jerusalem Baptist Church in Israel. He loved the land of our Lord. He prayed for the peace of Jerusalem. Allison's phone call was an answer to his prayers. He enthusiastically invited us to come to India.

Allison is our youngest daughter who attended the Anglican International School in Jerusalem. One of the requirements of the International Baccalaureate Program was to write a thesis on a compelling topic. After seeing the film, *Slum Dog Millionaire* she had been touched by the tragedy of childhood prostitution in Mumbai. A light went on. This was to be the theme of her thesis.

Our second daughter Emily had plans to visit India with a school mate. Of course, as concerned parents this did not seem like a safe idea. When her school mate's plans fell through, our two daughters decided to team up and go on their own to India. The questions of safety and costs went through our minds.

After much deliberation, we said that the only way we would allow them to go was that they work with an established well-known ministry. We thought of our friend Pete Phillips, who had served faithfully in an orphanage in India, before his passing away in 2006.
This was a possibility. Allison quickly did her own investigation. Thanks to Google, she found Rays of Hope ministry in Mumbai and quickly wrote Manoj.

When we received that phone call, we sensed in Manoj that his desire was that our whole family should come. The concern now was for the finances. This was a big undertaking.

My mother had gone to be with the Lord in January of 2010 and I knew there would be some inheritance. Perhaps this was the answer.

The Lord's timing was just right. The funds came through and off we were to the travel agent to make our plans for India.

In August of 2010, the four of us left Israel on a flight to Mumbai for a 3-week ministry adventure. First-hand experience is the best learning method. We were welcomed at the airport with a bouquet of flowers by Pastor Manoj. He said we would recognize him because he was short and dark.

Life in India had begun.

Just driving in the no-lane streets, with the weaving back and forth, and the constant sound of car horns, was a cultural first for us. Everything I had heard about India was true. Mumbai and its environs is a city of masses of people, constant activity, Hindu temples, mosques, churches, and cows using roads and highways as though they owned them.

For two weeks, we stayed in Manoj's home while he, his wife Priya and their children temporarily moved in with relatives. We had comfortable beds, a bucket for taking a shower with refreshing cool water, and a recently installed toilet (most of the bathrooms only have a hole in the ground). We felt privileged.

Our two weeks of ministry were challenging, varied, and joy-filled.

We were exposed to Asha-laya, the orphanage housing 40+ orphans. Fond of playing games, Billie and the girls had a wonderful time with

the children, while I played the guitar and sang. The older boys loved it when I taught them a few karate moves.

The HOPE Centre is a kindergarten/day care centre in the midst of a red-light slum near Mumbai. We were able to visit and minister to the children there. These were the children of the Commercial Sex workers in the area. It was a shocking experience to team up with Manoj and visit some of the "brothels" - to pray and preach the Gospel.

I think of Jesus who ministered to the Samaritan woman and His compassion for the adulteress condemned by the Pharisees.

Manoj is a great man of God with vision and compassion. It was a privilege to visit and share in various home meetings. We also met needy people and went to an Indian hospital to pray for a suffering child.

I was also able to preach in two of the six churches that Manoj has planted. This is amazing, since he is only 33 years old and he has also started an orphanage.
One day, Manoj showed us various pieces of

land around Mumbai that, Lord willing, could be purchased to begin the City of HOPE. This would be a complex for an orphanage, a school, a vocational training centre, a Bible institute and housing for the workers. Visiting this area was the highlight of our trip, and we prayed at the possible locations.

Our two weeks of ministry had come to an end. The last week was a holiday in which we toured the Golden Triangle (Delhi, Accra, and Jaipur).

Before flying back to Israel, we spent our last day with Manoj in Mumbai. At the airport we said our tear-filled good-byes.

In January, 2012 the Lord fulfilled Manoj's dream to visit the Holy Land. We travelled together through Israel. Besides seeing the sites, he shared and preached in various churches and home groups.

The Lord enabled us to raise funds for the work in India. The people who met Manoj were encouraged and blessed by the visit of this modern day "George Müller". My prayer is that God will do a work in India like he did in Bristol, England.

May the Lord continue to use Pastor Manoj and may the vision be fulfilled to the glory of God.

Dr. Al Nucciarone
Pastor Jerusalem Baptist Church
Jerusalem,Israel
July 2012

10

FROM THE AUTHOR

*P*astor Manoj Magar honoured us with a visit on Thursday, January 26, 2012. After the meal, he shared his amazing journey with God. We listened to how the Lord had called him, and prepared him to establish Rays of HOPE Ministries. Furthermore, he spoke about his dream and desire to build a City of HOPE.

"You're like a modern-day George Muller of Bristol!" I exclaimed. Manoj shyly shook his head. He didn't think he was.

"Someone should write a book about your life and the ministry!" I urged him.

"No, not right now," Manoj humbly responded. "Perhaps later. When the City of HOPE is ready."

He didn't like the idea of him being too much in the lime light.

"Petra can write the book," someone else at the table suggested. He mentioned the biography I had written about another servant of God.

"It will be a story that gives glory to our Heavenly Father," I promised.

That evening, nothing more was said about the book idea. However, after seeing the promotional DVD about the multi-faceted ministry, I knew in my heart that this story had to be told.

This year, 2012, **Rays of HOPE Ministries** celebrates its 10th anniversary. In this book you'll read how God had His hand upon Manoj's life, even before he was born. Called from the slums into His service, the young believer first learned how to serve others. Later, when Manoj became a preacher, he brought hope to the hopeless living in the slums. He discipled new believers and was instrumental in planting several churches.

God gave him a wonderful wife who shared his vision. Their personal sacrifices were great, but if necessary, they were willing to go the extra mile because they knew they were doing God's work. Honouring their

11

faith and their trust, God provided for the many orphans that came their way.

This story is about a group of humble Indian believers who live a life of serving and giving. This is not something that comes naturally - living an unselfish life is an art. These Christians regard others as more important than themselves. They look for ways to support, encourage, build up and stimulate. They follow in Christ's footsteps for,

"The Son of Man did not come to be served, but to serve, and to give His life as a ransom for many." Matthew 20:28

The staff of **Rays of HOPE Ministries** are role models who teach us that to be a servant of God, we must be a servant of people. They not only pursue a vertical holiness, but look around and are grieved over the corruption, the inequities, the hunger and misery and moral compromises they encounter daily. Their ministry is one of mercy to the miserable. Not only are they concerned for people and children in need, they try to do something about it.

Because of the tremendous needs in Mumbai, the daily challenges are enormous. But the workers of **Rays of HOPE Ministries** know they serve a mighty God who will provide all their needs. In His time.

I pray that this book not only will be a blessing to those who read it, but also a challenge. Especially today, when too many believers say, "Here I am, Lord… but send my sister." We can be God's ambassadors of mercy and love in a lost world, wherever we live.

Petra van der Zande
Jerusalem, August 2012

For God is not unjust to forget your work and labour of love which you have shown toward His name, in that you have ministered to the saints, and do minister. Hebrews 6:10

Migrant camp in Mumbai

Beautiful migrant children - what will their future be?

Will they end up like this mother and her baby, on the street, begging?

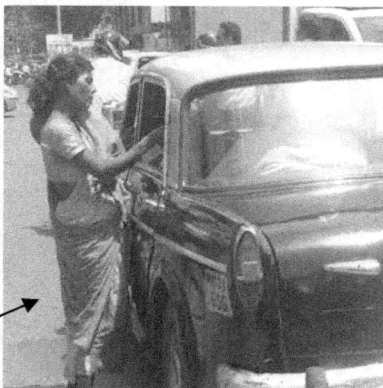

Or worse - become prostitutes?

Do they have a hope?

And a future?

INDIA

map:vernauclarmedia.org

History of India

The Republic of India, a country in South Asia, is a federal union of states. It is comprised of 28 states and 7 union territories, which are further subdivided into districts.
The country's motto is: "Truth Alone Triumphs".

The name India is derived from *Indus*, the Old Persian word for *Hindu*, Sanskrit *Sindhu*, the historic name for the Indus River.

India is 3,287,263 km² (1,269,219 sq mi), and has a population of 1,210,193,422. In 2011, they were the 7th largest country and the 2nd most populous country of the world.

The **National flag of India** is a horizontal rectangular tricolour of Deep saffron, white and India green, with a navy blue Ashok Chakra, a 24-spoke wheel, at its centre.

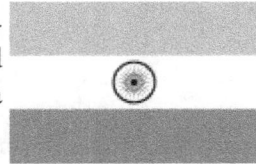

Hinduism, Buddhism, Jainism and Sikhism originated from India. The arrival of Zoroastrianism, Christianity and Islam helped shape the region's diverse culture.
Presently, Hinduism is the largest religion in India, followed by Islam. Christians, Sikhs, Buddhists, Jews and others are minorities.
East Indians, an ethnic Christian community, are descendants of converts of Portuguese catholic missionaries in the 13th century. The Marathi Christians are converts from 18th century
American and Anglican missionaries.

In ancient times, historic trade routes were used by many empires to transport India's commercial and cultural wealth from one continent to the other.

Gradually annexed by the British, in the early 18th century, India came under direct administration of the United Kingdom. India's modern age is considered to have begun between 1848 and 1885. After a long, mostly non-violent struggle for independence, led by Mahatma Gandhi, India became an independent nation in 1947.

In 1950, the completed constitution put in place a sovereign, secular and democratic republic.

The economic liberalization of the 1990's created a large urban middle class, which transformed India into one of the world's fastest growing economies.

India's traditional society is defined by a strict social hierarchy. Social classes are defined by castes. Many low-caste communities live in segregation, facing persecution and discrimination. Today, inter-caste marriage is on the rise, but mainly in urban India.

There are many changes due to female literacy and education, women at work, urbanization, the need for two-income families and influences from the media.

Eradication of poverty is considered to be a long-term goal of India's government. Since the 1950's, governmental and non-governmental organizations have initiated programs to alleviate poverty. Subsidizing food and other necessities, improving agricultural techniques and price support, promoting education and family planning have helped eliminate famines. However, malnutrition is on the rise.

There are many socio-economic challenges, as India has the largest concentration of people living below the (World banks international) poverty line of US $ 1.25 per day.

The Indian government specified poverty threshold is 32 rupees (about US $ 0.6) per day.

Many children are underweight and suffer from malnutrition; consequently, they are affected with diseases like diarrhoea, malaria and measles. The World Health Organisation (WHO) states that India has:

- 49% of the world's underweight children
- 34% of the world's stunted children
- 46% of the world's wasted children

Yearly, thousands of people die from drinking contaminated water or because of the polluted air.

Today, even the poorest families have cell-phones, access to electricity and television. Still, a lot needs to be done to help the growing number of disadvantaged families and their children.

India has highly qualified professionals in various fields. State of the art hospitals staffed with the best qualified doctors now also begin to attract medical tourism.

India's impressive economic prosperity has created a growing middle class. However, the gap between rich and poor is ever widening.

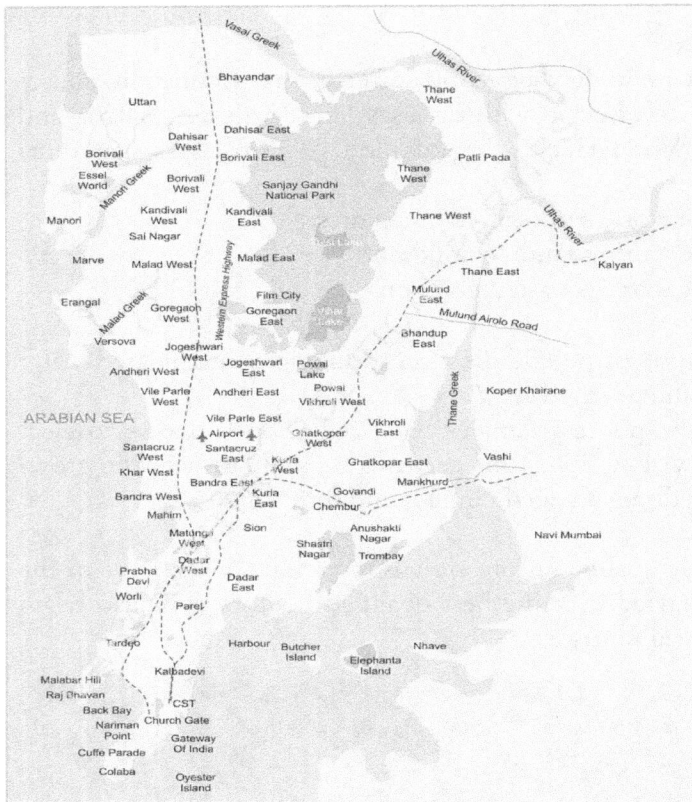

The **Gateway of India** is the most recognizable symbol of the city. It was built to commemorate the visit of the British Monarch King George V to India in 1911.

The history and origin of Mumbai (Bombay)

Initially, the group of seven islands on the Konkani coastline was occupied by Koli fishermen. Vasco da Gama, a Portuguese traveler, discovered the islands, which were captured by the Portuguese in 1534.

Deeming the area worthless, they gave them to Charles II of England as a wedding gift. Charles II leased them to the East India Company in 1668. They built docks, trading posts and a fort. Bombay became the gateway to India. In the 1800's the seven islands were coupled together. Bombay began to flourish with the opening of the Suez Canal in 1869.

In 1995, Bombay was renamed **Mumbai** after 'Mumbadevi', the patron goddess of Koli fisher folks and is now the capital of Maharashtra state. Mumbai is also the financial capital of India.

It houses the headquarters of all major banks, financial institutions, and insurance companies. The Bombay Stock Exchange, the oldest in Asia and largest of India is also located in the city.

'Bollywood' is the popular name for the Hindi-language film industry, based in Mumbai. Many films feature dialogue with Hinglish (Hindi-English).

83.2% of the Marathi people are Hindus. Hinduism plays an important role in Maharashtrian people's day-to-day life. Islam is the second biggest religion

in the state with more than 11 million adherents - over 10% of the population. 98% are Sunni Muslims.

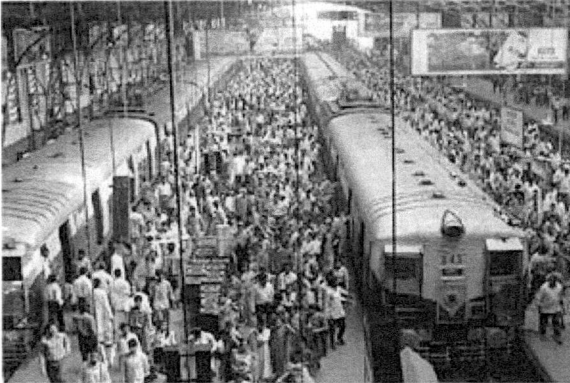

Mumbai Suburban Railway system carries more than 6.99 million commuters on a daily basis.
It has the highest passenger densities of any urban railway system in the world

Mumbai's business opportunities, as well as its potential to offer a higher standard of living, attract migrants from all over India. The city is a mix of many communities and cultures.

According to the 2001 census, Maharashtra, with a population of 96,752,247 inhabitants, is the second most populous state in India.

Mumbai's climate is tropical with moderate temperatures and a high level of humidity. The city has four seasons:

- Winter (from December till February)
- Summer (from March till May)
- Monsoon (from June till September)
- Post Monsoon (October till December)

The term 'Monsoon' was first used by the British to refer to the big seasonal winds blowing from the Bay of Bengal and the south-western Arabian Sea. These winds always bring heavy rainfall to the area.

Mumbai skyline

Slums
in
Mumbai

DEFINITION OF A SLUM

*D*efinition of a slum (zopadpattis)
A slum is a un-habitat, run down area of a city, characterized by substandard housing and squalor and lacking security. It is a maze of crowded, narrow alleyways, filled with barefoot and naked children.

Most of the inhabitants are very poor and disadvantaged. A slum building can be a simple shack or permanent and well maintained structure. Slums never undergo planning, lack infrastructure and facilities like water, sewage and drainage.
Because there is no garbage collection, rubbish accumulates in huge quantities. People face the brunt of natural (landslides, earthquakes, tropical storms) and man-made disasters, like fires.

Slums are characterized by urban decay, high rent rates, poverty, illiteracy and unemployment. They often are a breeding ground for social problems like crime, drugs, alcoholism, mental illnesses and suicide.

Different names:
- Shanty town: improvised shacks, made from scrap material.
- Skid row: urban area with a high homeless population
- Slum: based on socio-economic criteria, not racial, ethnic or religious.
- Chawl: multi storied tenement (higher quality than a slum). 80% of the housing consists of one room.
- Pavement dwellers: build their tent-like dwelling in city streets.

History of Mumbai's Slums

*B*efore India's independence, most slums were situated around the mills, where the workers lived in one room-tenements. In 1947, about 16,500 people lived on one sq. mile in the city of Bombay.

After 1950, there was an increase in migration to the big cities. Slums increased to such an extent that by 1980, half of Mumbai's population lived in slums.

Even today, the rags-to-riches dream brings many people to Mumbai. Few however, escape the grinding poverty and hopelessness. For most people living in the slum the dream remains a disappointing illusion.

Slums are a fact of life for most of the middle-class people of Mumbai.

In 2012, 60% (about 7 million people) of Mumbai's population lived in slums. Some even call the city "Slumbay" .

The slum areas encroach onto airport land, and often sit cheek by jowl with apartments that cost a few thousand dollars rent a month.

The infant mortality rate is high in Mumbai because of constant migration, lack of water, sewage and solid waste facilities, a lack of transportation, pol-

lution and housing shortage.
The general hospitals are overcrowded and under-resourced. The
poor often have to go to un-
qualified private doctors.

Water is always too little, or too
much. During the monsoon season, the slums are often sub-
merged in knee deep water. The
contaminated river water, where
most of the slum's waste ends up, causes many diseases.
Rats and mice are also a part of life in the slums.

In 1985, the "slum up-gradation project" offered secure long-term
legal plot tenure, on the basis that the people invested in their housing. This project only targeted 10-12% of the slum population, and
didn't regard those who had no home at all.

The slum economy consists of street vending, drug dealing, domestic work and prostitution. Many people are recycling trash as a way
of income. Rag pickers work 10-12 hours a day, to earn about $ 1-
$ 1.50 per day.

The Major Slums of Mumbai

1. Dharavi
2. Baiganwadi
3. Ghatkopar
4. Govadi

1. Dharavi
This area of 535 acres (217 ha) is located on prime property in the
middle of India's financial capital. The former island, which used to

be inhabited by Koli fishermen, was surrounded by swamps. Gradually, the swamps filled with coconut leaves, rotten fish and human waste. Deprived of their living, the Kolis began to bootleg liquor.

The drained swamps invited new communities to move in. Dharavi now has more than one million people, many of whom are second and even third generation. The location and poor drainage make the area vulnerable to floods during the wet season.

Migrants who made Dharavi their home were potters from Gujarat and people working in the tanning and leather industry. Today, the slum has a flourishing pottery, textile and recycling industry. There are about 5,000 businesses and 15,000 single room factories.

18,000 people are living together on 1 acre (0.4 ha). Fifteen people share a 300 sq. feet room with numerous mice. Because there is only one toilet per 1,440 residents, people use the

Mahim Creek (local river) as public toilet. Even though there is inadequate drinking water in Dharavi, many of the illegally built houses have a colour TV and cable connection to watch their favourite soap operas.

26

2. Baiganwadi

This largest waste dumping ground is home to many immigrants from Bihar and Utar Pradesh and illegals from Bangla-Desh, who are packed together in 10x15 ft. rooms. Because there is no proper water supply, many resort to illegal water connections.

3. Ghatkopar

Is home to around 100,000 people, who prefer to call themselves a 'colony'.

In 2000, many people were killed during a land-slide.

4. Govandi

This area consists of shanty type structures, open sewers and garbage filled passages. Bonded child labour is rife here.

Thousands of "Zari factories" force 6-14 young boys to work and live in miserable conditions.

Zari factory

27

LIFE IN THE SLUM

$\mathcal{M}$umbai is a city where traffic never stops and horns always honk.

It is early morning when Dharavi, in the heart of the financial district, wakes up.

From the vast mass of huts and alleyways sounds of devotional singing are heard. This is followed by a rush of water. Many homes now have their own (often illegal) water tap.

A woman opens a hose and washes down the filth from her entrance.

People who don't have their own tap, have to walk a mile (1.6 km) to get water for cleaning and cooking. In the past, local goons only filled the woman's buckets from the spigot after she paid them. Slum dwellers often find themselves at the mercy of land mafia who are in charge of the water and electricity.

Nowadays, government sponsored water projects help the local people to obtain uncontaminated water.

In the wide lanes, cab drivers coax their battered Fiats to life, while the potter's kilns belch black smoke into the air. In the mucky industrial canal, the recyclers are already hard at work.

Barefooted children play with sticks and pieces of rubbish beside a stream of black water. Filth runs between shacks that have been built from discarded doors and scrap metal. Even in daylight, the rats show themselves.

The only colours in this place are the washed bright clothes hanging to dry. Through an open door, one can look inside the small, dingy rooms, which are decorated with religious pictures or Bollywood stars.

Men push heavy laden carts, and the recyclers sift their 'treasures'.

Another day has begun in Dharavi.

INDIA'S CASTE SYSTEM

$\mathcal{I}$n ancient India there developed a social system in which people were divided into separate closed communities. These communities are known in English as castes. Hinduism originated the caste system, but it has affected the whole of Indian society. The caste system in the religious form is basically a simple division of society in which there are four castes arranged in a hierarchy and below them the outcast. But socially the caste system was more complicated, with many more castes and sub-castes and other divisions. In all, there are 3,000 castes in India.

Legally the government disallows the practice of the caste system but it has a policy of affirmative discrimination of the backward classes.

There are four castes (Varnas) in Hindu society, each with assigned duties, responsibilities and privileges.

- Brahmins - the learned, educated, Vedic priests
- Kshatriyas - the kings, governors and soldiers
- Vaishyas – the cattle herders, farmers and merchants
- Sudras – labourers, artisans and service providers

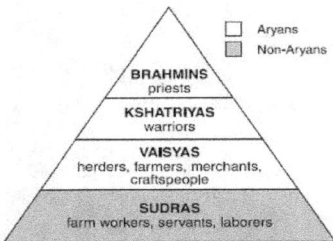

Source: *Guide to the Essentials of World History*, Prentice Hall, 1999 (adapted)

Brahmins are on the highest rung of the social hierarchy, and Sudras are on the lowest.

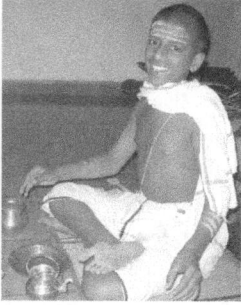
Brahmin boy

Dalit woman - an outcast

Sudra farmer

THE "UNTOUCHABLES"

The untouchability feature in the caste system is one of the cruellest features of the system. Many see it as one of the strongest racist phenomenon in the world.

In the Indian society, those who worked in ignominious, polluting and unclean occupations were seen as polluting peoples and were therefore considered as untouchables. The untouchables had almost no rights in the society. In some regions they were treated harshly, in other regions more leniently.

In the 1500s, the rulers of today's Maharashtra state forbade 'untouchables' to enter Poona, then the capital city, between 3.00 pm and 9.00 am. During this time period, their bodies were likely to cast long shadows, which could fall on a Brahmin and pollute him.

An 'untouchable' had to carry an earthen pot around his neck so his spittle would not pollute the earth.

They also had to wear a black thread either around their neck or wrist for ready identification. In other places they could be wearing a horn for the same reason.

"Untouchables" 1946

The untouchables were not allowed to:

- touch people from the four Varnas.
- enter houses of the higher Varnas.
- enter the temples.
- use the same wells used by the Varnas.
- and were compelled to sit at a distance from the four Varnas during public meetings.

In regions where the attitude towards the untouchables was more severe, not only touching them was seen as polluting, but even contact with their shadow was unthinkable.

Accidental contact with an untouchable "defiled" a member of the Varnas. He then had to immerse or wash himself with water to be purified. In strict societies, especially among the 'Twice Born' (the three top Varnas) when touched, he had to go through a religious ceremony to purify himself from the pollution.

Sometimes untouchables were beaten or even murdered for interacting with Varnas.

The 'untouchables' constitute 15% of the total population of the sub-continent. They are also called Depressed Classes, Scheduled Castes or Scheduled Tribes.

"Harijans" Mahatma Gandhi used to call them – "children of God".

Today, the untouchables are called "Dalits". The Sanskrit word means "ground", "suppressed", "crushed", or "broken to pieces". According to Victor Premasager, the term expresses their "weakness, poverty and humiliation at the hands of the upper castes in the Indian society."

Dalits are involved in leatherwork, butchering, or removal of rubbish, animal carcasses, and waste.

They also work as manual labourers cleaning streets, latrines, and sewers.

Mother Theresa - loving and caring for the outcasts

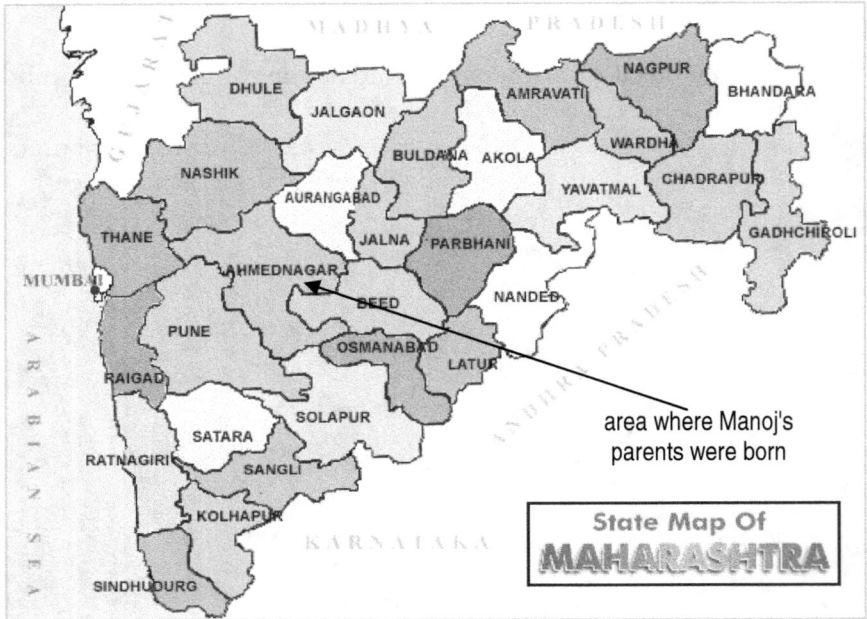

State Map Of MAHARASHTRA

area where Manoj's parents were born

MAHAR is the largest scheduled caste group in the Indian state of Maharashtra. Traditionally, the community was made to live on the outskirts of villages. They were the village watchman, messengers, wall menders, adjudicators of boundary disputes, street sweepers, and carcass removers.

Working as agricultural labourers, they sometimes held some land, though they were not primarily farmers. During the nineteenth century, many Mahars converted to Christianity through the outreaches of American and British evangelists. William Carey, a British missionary, was instrumental in translating the Bible into Marathi. During the 20th century a number of Mahars converted to Buddhism.

As the collective consciousness of the Mahar grew, significant numbers of their communities began to leave their traditional villages and move into the urban centers of India in search of better employment and educational opportunities. In urban centers, caste origins were less obvious and less important in public life.

The Story of Manoj Magar - Servant of God

Family background

Maharashtra, the largest state in western India, is subdivided into smaller districts. Ahmednagar, one of them, has many rural areas. Manoj's grand-parents and father were born in a village called Yeli-Jambhali.

The British conquest over the Maratha Empire opened the door to Christianity and the first Protestant Christian mission opened in 1831. Marathi, the national language of the state Maharashtra, was spoken in rural villages. Schools also taught Hindi, but no English.

Manoj's family belonged to the "Mahars" - a caste which was also called the 'untouchables'.

In the 1960's many mass evangelistic meetings were held to reach the lower casts of whom the untouchables were the poorest of the poor. Benefits given by the missionaries prompted many to convert to Christianity.

It did not appeal to Manoj's family, who were devout Hindus. Their goddess was Mohata Devi, a specific idol that was worshipped in that region.

"I'm going to Mumbai," Manoj's father Tukaram told his parents in 1972. "I'll be able to find employment there. And then I can support a wife."

Mumbai Municipality hired him as a labourer and two years later the young man returned to his village to get married.

HINDUISM

Hinduism is the predominant religion of the Indian subcontinent. It is formed of diverse traditions and has no single founder. There is no "unified system of belief encoded in declaration of faith or a creed".

According to an Indian theologian, "Hinduism is not 'just a faith', but in itself is related to the union of reason and intuition. It cannot be defined, but only to be experienced."

Hinduism is often called the "oldest living religion" or the "oldest living major religion" in the world. Being a traditional way of life, Hinduism is often defined as a religious tradition.

Hindu themes
- ***Dharma*** (ethics/duties) – That which upholds, supports or maintains the regulatory order of the universe.
- ***Samsara*** (The continuing cycle of birth, life, death and rebirth)
- ***Karma*** (action and subsequent reaction) – deed, cause and effect.
- **Moksha** (liberation from *samsara*)
- Various **Yogas** (paths or practices)
- ***Reincarnation*** – after death, the soul or spirit is believed to return in a new human body, animal or plant.

Many Hindus engage in religious rituals on a daily basis, mostly observed at home. At dawn, a devout Hindu first bathes, and then worships before a family shrine. He lights a lamp, offers food before the images of deities, reads from religious scripts, sings devotional hymns, meditates, chants mantras, recites scriptures etc.

Hindus believe in the importance of sacrifice and merit, gained through the performance of charity or good works, that will accumulate over time and reduce sufferings in the next world.

The groom took his bride, Muktabai, to live in Vadala, a slum in Mumbai. Their first 'home' was made from rags and plastic sheets. Later, they moved to Ramabai Nagar in Ghatkopar - a slum area that was notorious for its crime and illegal activities.

Tukaram worked as a labourer of the BMC (Bombay Municipal Corporation) water department, while Muktabai was a housewife. She cooked on a firewood stove and bought their food at the local market.

"We've saved enough money to buy tin sheets for the walls," Tukaram said one day. "And I can even build a roof!"
Muktabai was also happy when they had saved enough money to buy a kerosene stove.

Two public toilets served the Ghatkopar population of thousands of people.
Halfway between the toilets was the public water tap.
Every morning, Muktabai patiently stood in line with a bucket or container to receive their daily ration of water.

Preferring to live their own, quiet lives, Manoj's parents tried to stay clear of the goons and criminals operating in the slum.

37

Two years after their marriage, Manohar was born by way of a Cae-sarean section.

In rural areas women give birth at home. In the city, women go to the hospital. The usual stay is 24 hours, unless there are complica-tions or after a C-section. Government hospitals and those run by local municipalities treat patients for free. Patients only pay a nomi-nal fee for medications and utilities they need.

It was a miracle Muktabai survived the birth of her first child. She was two weeks in hospital to recuperate.

"After this very difficult delivery, you better have no more chil-dren," the doctor advised her.

However, three years later, in 1978, another baby was conceived. Examining Muktabai, the doctor shook his head.

"You are not strong enough to have this baby," he told her. "I will give you medication for an abortion."

But whatever he did, or tried, the baby could and would not be aborted. God's unseen hand was already upon the life of this un-born child – He wanted the child to live!

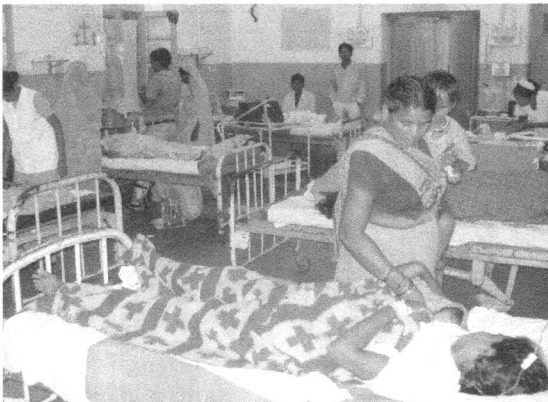

The pregnancy went well and there were no complications when Manoj was born on February 4, 1979

After two days, Mukta-bai was released from the Municipal Hospital in Mumbai and brought baby Manoj home.

illustrative photo

38

CHAWLS vs. HIGHRISE

Chawl is a name for a type of building found in India. They are often 4 to 5 stories with about 10 to 20 tenements, referred to as **kholis**, (literally 'rooms') on each floor.

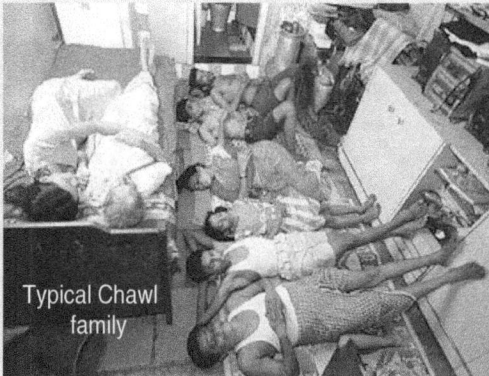

In the early 1900s, cotton mill owners and private builders created chawls to house the majority of its urban poor. Many people migrated to the city because of its booming cotton mills and overall strong economy.

A usual tenement in a chawl consists of one room that functions both as a living and sleeping space, and a kitchen that doubles as a dining room. Often, the kitchen serves as a bedroom for a newly married couple, to give them some degree of privacy. Average rents run about Rs. 1,000 ($ 20) per month.

Families share a common block of latrines - each block usually contains 4 to 5 latrines. Tenements with private bathrooms are highly sought after and cost 50% more than the price of a normal chawl.

Typical Chawl family

People living in a chawl have little privacy. Due to the close nature of the quarters, trivial news and gossip travel quickly. On the other hand, the community has support networks akin to familial relationships.

City developers are always seen as a threat to those living in the chawls. The occupants resist change and fear losing out on the unity, togetherness, security, camaraderie, cultural essence and ethos.
Those forcibly evicted from their chawl to a high-rise building because of redevelopment of the area, mostly miss having contact with other people.

The lack of a courtyard or open space and the need to travel a long-distance to play cricket doesn't help either. Often, the new building is poorly constructed and elevators break down easily.

Even though moving to these new premises provides better living standards, the chawl community feels they've lost more than they gained.

Early childhood

From birth till age five, Manoj suffered from severe asthma, for which he had to take different medications on a daily basis.

"Don't expect him to live for long," the doctor warned his worried parents.

Desperate to save her sick child, Muktabai took the little boy to Hindu temples, ritual sites and witch doctors.

Manoj grew up amongst relatives and neighbours who were addicted to alcohol. The slum society struggled with the cycle of poverty. Alcoholism not only made it worse, it destroyed the lives of families, wives and children. Every slum family had someone with an alcohol problem. The illegally sold liquor was dangerous and harmful to the body.

Tukaram too was addicted to this alcohol, and Manoj often heard his mother complain that there was no food in the house. Instead of bringing the daily wage of around $ 2 (Rs. 90) home to buy food or clothes, he spent most of it (Rs. 70) in the liquor store. Those were the days Manoj went to bed hungry, because there was no money to buy food.

Because of his severe asthma, he could hardly breathe, and this affected his body temperature – the little boy couldn't stay warm.

"You take him along," Muktabai told her husband. "I don't know what to do with him."

On his way to jobs, Tukaram often gave the little child liquor to drink - it was the only way he knew to keep his son warm. Before the age of five, Manoj had tasted all kinds of liquor – the legal and illegal kinds.

The Ghatkopar slum was regularly visited by a group of Roman Catholic nuns. Not only did they give humanitarian aid and practical help, but they also shared the Gospel.

Muktabai gradually had become more open towards this other religion, Christianity.

"Jesus is just one of the gods," she told the nun. "He is part of the many statues of gods and goddesses we worship."

Illustrative photo

Even though the nun explained the Gospel to her, Muktabai continued to be a devout Hindu.

One day, during morning devotions, Muktabai prayed to the statue of Jesus standing amongst the other household idols, "If you are alive, and if you save my child, we will believe in You and I will give this child to You."

During another outreach in the slum, Muktabai told one of the nuns about Manoj's fragile health.

"Do you mind if I pray for the little boy?" the nun asked.
Muktabai had tried everything, so she decided it wouldn't hurt if a Christian prayed for her Hindu child.

42

God had a special plan for Manoj's life. Honouring the faith of this nun – He healed the five year-old boy from his asthma!

From Youth till Teenager

Manoj grew stronger every day and was able to go to the slum school. By now, he had another brother - Mangesh.

Like all children, Manoj loved to watch television. Lacking electricity and having no TV, the family went to a neighbour or friend to watch. Not everyone was happy when they came over, and often, Manoj and his brothers were forced to stand outside the house and watch TV from there.

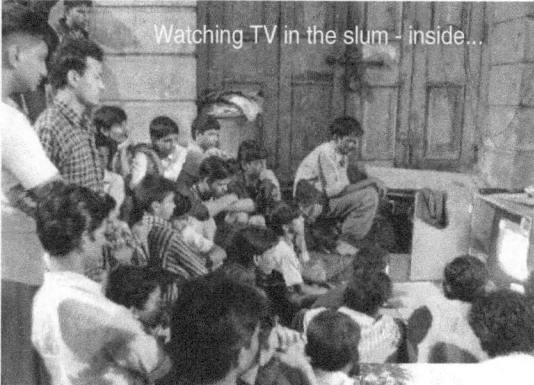

Watching TV in the slum – inside...

Another option was to go to the nearby school ground to watch television. The area was packed with about 100 people sitting on the ground.

Adults always got the best places and Manoj was often too far away to see the screen.

... or outside

43

By the time Manoj was 12 years old, their house had been hooked up to the electricity grid.

"Look what I bought from a colleague!" Father proudly showed a used, 15" Black and White, TV set. Manoj and his brothers were so excited and proud that they now had their own TV set!

Having a regular job, his father brought in enough money for the family to have three meals a day. They had rice or curry, and barley bread. Sometimes there was an egg or they ate the cheap local fish. Being Hindus, they would never eat beef, and chicken was

Hindu woman feeding a holy cow

considered a luxury. Therefore, most of the meals were vegetarian.

Indian Cuisine

Indian cuisine is known for its delicate use of herbs and spices and for its *tandoori* preparations. The *tandoor,* a clay oven used in India for almost 5,000 years, grills meats to an "uncommon succulence" and produces the puffy flatbread known as *naan.* The staple foods are wheat (predominantly in the north), rice (especially in the south and the east), and lentils. Many spices which have worldwide appeal are native to the Indian subcontinent, while chili pepper, introduced by the Portuguese, is also widely used by Indians. Common traditional eating customs include meals taken on or near the floor, caste- and gender-segregated dining, and lack of cutlery in favour of the right hand or a piece of *roti* (South-Asian word for bread).

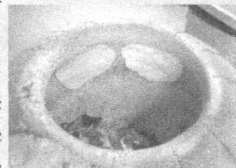

During the main meal, the family drank boiled water. Tea (with sugar) was part of breakfast and drunk in the evening.

Noticing that his mother treated his older and younger brother with more care, Manoj felt rejected. Comparing the leftovers on his plate with the best portions his mother had given his brothers, the young boy became sad.

I'm taken for granted, Manoj thought bitterly. *And I hate it when I have to wear my brother's clothes.* He wanted to experience the joy of having something new. *One day, when I can live on my own, I will sever all ties with my family,* the deeply hurt boy vowed.

From grade 1-7 Manoj went to Ghatkopar's municipal local school, where the education standard was low. Foreign languages were only taught after 5th grade, and even then, most of the teachers didn't know much about the subject anyway. The children learned the foreign alphabet, a few words and that was it.

Illustrative photo

Illustrative photo

School days were divided into two shifts: morning and afternoon. Morning school (from 7th grade) was from 7 a.m. till about 1 p.m.

After finishing his homework, Manoj had to do his share of household chores. Then it was time to play with his friends.

Besides his school uniform, the youngster only had a few sets of clothes. Shoes were a luxury his parents couldn't afford, so he wore only sandals.

45

The alcohol addiction had forced Tukaram to take many loans. These had to be paid back, which didn't leave money for extras. Mother could barely make it through the month.

"Can we please go and visit Untie?" Manoj often begged his mother. *At least I will get something to eat,* he thought.

The acquaintance, who came from the same village as their parents, always had plenty of food, and different fruits that he had never tasted. It pained him to see precious fruit left to rot in the basket.

Illustrative photo

"Here they come again!" a friend warned Manoj when the evangelists entered the slum.

"I hate them!" twelve year-old Manoj responded.

In a short period of time, Manoj was involved in two major accidents. One day, he was hit by a speeding taxi, and miraculously survived. Another day, his mother took Manoj and another boy shopping. They were riding in an auto riksha when the three-wheeled vehicle crashed, rolled over three times, and ended upside down. Both accidents should have been deadly, but God miraculously saved them. They survived, and without major injuries.

When Ghatkopar's "City of the Lord Church" assembled to worship in the classroom of the local school, the boys were ready to disturb the meeting.

This went on for quite some time.

"Did you see so-and-so?" a friend asked Manoj one day. "He has become a Christian, and his life is totally changed!"

Manoj grudgingly had to admit this was true. "And the one who used to be a tough criminal," he said. "That man has become gentle!" He shook his head in disbelief. "I want to know this Jesus," he admitted. "I'm not interested in religion, but want to know what He is about."

Illustrative photo

Ghatkopar's local church organized a Vacation Bible School and all slum children were invited.

"Are you going?" Manoj asked his friends.
"Of course!" they responded.

Illustrative photo

It was only because of them that he participated. Manoj had to admit - he liked the ten-day program.

"You all are invited to come to the Sunday service," the teacher said.
"Are you going?" Manoj asked his friends.
"No way!"

Even though his friends were not interested, Manoj felt an inner urge to go to the meeting.
The Holy Spirit convinced him he was a sinner who needed salvation. In May 1991, Manoj accepted Christ as his Lord and Saviour and made a commitment to walk with Him.

Apprehensive about his parent's reaction, he knew he had to tell them.

"I've become a Christian!"

To his relief, they were not opposed. "That is good, son," Tukaram responded. Being devout Hindus, they saw it as one of the many ways to god.

For most of his friends, the Vacation Bible School had been a nice break, but they didn't believe in that Jesus. Eventually, many of Manoj's childhood friends ended up dying of AIDS or became alcoholics. Without a job, and no money, they faced a bleak future.
Monahar, Manoj's older brother, had also come to the Lord. Together, the two teenagers shared the gospel with their parents.

"Please, come with us to the Sunday service," Manoj asked.
Over time, both parents became more interested.

"Tell us more about this Jesus Christ you two keep talking about with so much passion," they said.

God did a miracle in this troubled Hindu family. By God's grace, Tukaram was able to give up alcohol. He now is a committed Christian who walks with God. The devout Hindu responded to Jesus' call, and was set free!

"Grandmother is demon possessed." Yeli-Jambhali's villagers were convinced she was. Many Hindus believed god communicated through Manoj's grandmother by manifestations and during special occasions.

"She is a goddess!" People from surrounding areas visited the woman to ask her for a special blessing.

Being a devout Hindu, Grandmother had worshipped idols all of her life. She didn't know any better. That was, until the day the old woman lay on her deathbed and Manoj and his family shared the Gospel with her.

"Grandmother, you have to accept Jesus as your Saviour!" they urged her. Both Tukaram and his brother prayed with and for their dying mother. They believed God forgave her sins, and she was set free. Two days later, she went to be with the Lord.

FOLLOWING JESUS

*D*esiring to serve the Lord, twelve-year-old Manoj became actively involved in the local church. On Sunday morning, he collected the key to the school and prepared the classroom for the morning service. He swept the floor, cleaned the benches and desks, and arranged the seats for the service. During the meeting, he served as an usher. After the service, Manoj cleaned everything up again and returned the key to the school authorities.

He loved every minute of it - it was a joy to serve God in such a practical way.

During the week the young believer attended the Bible study and thought it an honour to carry the bag of the Sunday school teacher. By performing these humble and practical tasks, Manoj learned to serve and carry many responsibilities.

Marathi Bible

Serving the Lord with ALL of his heart

*I*n 1992, God gave Manoj a vision of future events: he would go to the nations, and he would speak to many people. Too young to understand the vision, Manoj kept quiet. But there was another reason why he was reluctant to tell others about it.

I don't want to serve God full-time, he thought. *I don't want to live a difficult life!* He had seen the conditions under which local full-time ministers lived. *They struggle financially and often face violent opposition.*
He didn't want to go through all that pain. *I want to study further, build a career and establish myself!* he decided. *I can be both prosperous and a good Christian.*

For two years, the Lord continued to speak to Manoj's heart. He used different people to confirm the calling, even people whom Manoj did not know. God used men and women who sometimes spoke a word of prophecy, or a prophetic prayer over him.
Sometimes they sensed the Lord's guidance while praying for him, and then shared their feelings with the young believer. All the confirmations he received were in line with what God had been putting on his heart.
In May 1994, Manoj stood at crossroads. *I have to decide what to do next*, he knew. *Higher education means following my personal direction - the way of the flesh. Obeying God's calling, means following the Lord's direction.*
The emotional and spiritual struggle was intense and exhausting.

Sunday morning, during his devotional time, Manoj prayed, "God, I know that You are speaking to me. You want me to serve You, but I need your confirmation. I have to make a decision. I want to know what I must do next."
Opening his Bible he read Isaiah 60 and 61. Through these verses, the clear voice of God spoke about Manoj's calling. *It is like a friend*

speaking to a friend – so personal, and so clear, he thought.

However, even though the young man knew God wanted him to serve Him, his human side wasn't quite willing to give in.

Again, he prayed, "If this is truly from You, Lord, and if You want me to serve You, I still need a confirmation. I want to hear it!"

That Sunday morning, as he had faithfully done over the past two years, Manoj prepared the school building for the church service. With his heart in turmoil and because of the many thoughts whirling through his head, Manoj couldn't concentrate on the worship. He saw himself standing at a crossroad, struggling and debating which direction to take.

"Let's read Isaiah 60 and 61." The local pastor opened his Bible. Manoj's heart skipped a beat when he began to preach on the same verses he had read that morning!

"The Spirit of the Lord GOD is upon Me, Because the LORD has anointed Me To preach good tidings to the poor; He has sent Me to heal the brokenhearted, To proclaim liberty to the captives, And the opening of the prison to those who are bound; To proclaim the acceptable year of the LORD, And the day of vengeance of our God; To comfort all who mourn, To console those who mourn in Zion, To give them beauty for ashes, The oil of joy for mourning, The garment of praise for the spirit of heaviness; That they may be called trees of righteousness, The planting of the LORD, that He may be glorified."

The same verses. The same message. *This is for you!* God spoke to Manoj's heart.

Illustrative photo

In the middle of the sermon, the teenager fell on his knees and surrendered his life to God.

There and then, he made a new and fresh commitment to serve Him.

That decision had many consequences. Not only did he have to let go of his personal desires, but his parents didn't like the idea that their son was going into full-time ministry.

"But this is what I want to do!" Manoj was absolutely sure. "I'm giving up my personal plans and desires," he stated. "I'm going to serve the Lord with ALL of my heart!"

God's Training Ground

The pastor of the local church looked at the young man who asked to speak with him.

"I want to be in full-time ministry," Manoj said.

"What can you do? A fifteen-year-old teenager?" the pastor objected. "How can you be useful?"

"God spoke to me!" Manoj was not going to give up. "I promised to serve Him."

In the end, realizing the youngster was serious about his calling, the pastor allowed Manoj to join the team.

Between 1994 and 2000, the young believer learned to serve God by humbly serving others.

He cleaned toilets, houses, the pastor's office, washed cars, carried Bible boxes and stamped gospel tracts.

He felt it a privilege to carry the bags of the team leaders he worked with.

During those early years, Manoj never had an opportunity to preach or pray with people. His main activities were simple tasks through which he served others. Manoj did it with joy.

But it wasn't easy. Being the youngest (and shortest) of a team of about 40

Illustrative photo

ministry workers, to Manoj they looked like giants. They always called him *"Chintu"* (shorty). The insult humiliated him and reminded him of the way his father always treated him.

"I never trust short guys," Tukaram used to say to him. "They are unreliable."

The knowledge that his father didn't trust him, hurt Manoj deeply.

> If we are faithful to God in little things, we shall gain experience and strength that will be helpful to us in the more serious trials of life.
> Hudson Taylor

Years later, he understood that those years were God's training ground for him. The Lord used it as a workshop to prepare and train Manoj for his future ministry. It was a very important period in which he learned about commitment, responsibilities and ministering to the local church.

It was in 1999 that God began to unfold the mission which He had shown Manoj seven years previously. That vision was **Rays of HOPE Ministries** (RHM).

But again, the idea was too big and overwhelming for Manoj. He could neither grasp nor understand it. *How can I respond to this calling?* he wondered. *I would rather serve God in the local church.* He wanted to remain in this comfortable ministry where he had nothing to worry about. Because he received a very small allowance each month, he didn't have to pray for funds to come in. *Serving God through the local church is a sure and stable position. I like to keep it that way,* he decided.

Again the Lord spoke to Manoj.

"I want you to step out in faith and begin pioneering the RHM!"

The young man wasn't ready to take that step yet, and God, in His mercy, had patience with him.

But He didn't leave His servant alone.

53

BIBLE SCHOOL LESSONS

Three years later, in 2001, Manoj realized he had reached another crossroads. In order to decide which step to take next, he felt the need to leave Mumbai for a while. *I have to find a place where I can wait upon the Lord,* he thought.

Only by being away from his present place of ministry, would he be able to evaluate his decisions. *I must be absolutely sure which direction God is leading me.*

"Lord, You have to give me instructions about what to do next," he prayed.

In December that year, Manoj informed his pastor, family and friends, "I want to go for six months to a Bible School in the south of India."

"Sounds like you want to follow the desires of the flesh," someone said.

"You're committing foolishness," another believer remarked.

One of the leaders of the church even said that he would have a hard time there. "You're going to fail," he predicted. "You'll have to beg in order to return to Mumbai."

Truth to be told, Manoj himself wasn't so sure about this step either. He didn't have any resources, and there was no one to accompany him. Besides having no friends in the south, he had no one to support him financially.

The only thing he did have was this inner conviction, this calling, and God's promise that He was leading him. Even though it seemed foolish, even to himself, Manoj could do nothing but obey. Even if this meant that he had to go against the wishes and advice of his family, the local church, the pastors and his friends.

Finding himself totally alone, Manoj knew that God was with him.

The **Indian rupee** (sign:₹ ; code: **INR**) is the official currency of the Republic of India. The modern rupee is subdivided into 100 paise (singular *paisa*). The Indian rupee symbol ₹ was officially adopted in 2010.

Bank notes are available in nominal values of 5, 10, 20, 50, 100, 500 and 1000 rupees. Coins of the rupee are available in 1, 2, 5 and 10. Paise coins of the rupee have nominal values of 50, and lower denominations have been officially withdrawn.

Taking a step of faith, he enrolled in the Bible School.

From childhood, Manoj had been saving money. Even from the small church allowance he received he managed to save a little. Rs. 10 ($ 0.5) a month wasn't much, but at least it was something to add to his saving account!

By the time he went to the Bible School, Manoj had Rs. 8,000 (about $ 200) in his bank account. Having all this money gave him a sense of security. *It will help me start the ministry,* he thought. *There is no need to ask for financial support. With this money I can travel around, do outreaches and organize activities,* he reasoned.

But God wanted Manoj to learn an important lesson.
During his first week in Bible school, God spoke clearly and unmistakingly, "Empty your bank account!"
It was too much for Manoj.

"Lord, I followed your voice and instruction," he protested. "I've given up everything to follow You. I'm here, all alone. I don't know where I'm going or what will happen next. I'm willing to obey Your calling on my life. But now You are asking too much of me."
The Rs. 8,000 was the only money he had. No longer did he receive an allowance. He didn't have a mission board, nor support from friends. Manoj trusted this money to help him start the Lord's ministry.

That first month in Bible School became a miserable time for Manoj. Not only did he have to empty his bank account, God also spoke to him about the grudge he held towards his parents. How well he remembered the rejection and loneliness he suffered as a young child.

You have to repent and ask forgiveness, the Lord told him. *Only then will you be able to start Rays of HOPE Ministries.*

With a heavy heart, Manoj dialled his parent's phone number. Crying bitterly, he told them that God didn't want him to hold a grudge against them.

"Can you please forgive me?" he cried. "You are my parents. And I love you."
Of course they wholeheartedly forgave him.

It was then and there that Manoj decided that he would always look after his parents. God wanted him to bless them back for looking after him, as well as they could, at that time. *In their old age, I will be responsible for them,* he decided. After the phone call, it felt as if a heavy burden had been lifted.

However, the bank account issue remained unresolved.
Even though Manoj tried to ignore it, with each passing day the inner voice kept growing. God's voice became louder and stronger.
I want you to sow the money into the Bible School, God told him, over and over again.
"All right!" Unable to bear the pressure any longer, Manoj sat

down to write the cheque. Staring at the piece of paper, he still wasn't ready to hand it over to the director of the Bible school.

"I can't. Not yet." He put the cheque in his Bible for safe keeping.

For seven days, he took it with him to classes. The cheque was still in his Bible when he returned to the dormitory. The young man just couldn't release his last and only security. Not yet.

On Friday, Manoj decided to fast. While worshipping in the prayer room, he felt God's presence. *Like a friend visiting a friend,* he thought. It was as if the world around him stopped, and Manoj was suspended in time. An overwhelming peace and calmness entered his soul. And it was in this stillness that he heard God's voice loud and clear,

"Do what I told you: go, empty your bank account!"

Manoj fell on his knees. "I do my best to obey you!" he argued. "Yes Lord, I heard you!" Repeating what he had told the Lord before, he added, "I'm willing to trust You. I have trusted You all this time, Lord. Even now, as You ask me to make this sacrifice, this very amount. The last and only money that I have. I'm willing to give it out, to sow it, and trust that You will take care of my every personal need. And of every need related to my ministry. Never will I ask anyone for money, or to supply my personal needs. Rather, I will pray and seek You. You will make sure that all my needs are met."

Grabbing his Bible, with the cheque, Manoj went in search of the chairman of the Bible School. The man and his wife were just on their way to the dining area. Many of the 450 students attending the Bible school approached

> Faith does not operate in the realm of the possible. There is no glory for God in that which is humanly possible. Faith begins where man's power ends.
> George Müller

the chairman with all kinds of requests, which often involved finances.

"I would like to talk to you about something." Manoj told the chairman.

Expecting he was going to ask for money, their faces fell.

Unable to speak, Manoj opened his Bible and handed them the cheque. "God told me to do this." He almost choked on the words.

He didn't want to wait to see their reaction. Neither did he have the courage to give an explanation. Manoj fled to the dormitory.

When his heartbeat returned to normal, Manoj was surprised to experience an overwhelming peace. He had expected to feel sad, but instead, he bubbled over with joy! His confidence in God had been restored. "You are with me, Lord!" he knew. "And You are going to see me through!"

And from that day onwards, God has proven His faithfulness by providing for every personal and ministry need, without Manoj having to ask people for money.

FAITH

has nothing to do with feelings or with impressions, with improbabilities or with outward experiences. If we desire to couple such things with faith, then we are no longer resting on the Word of God, because faith needs nothing of the kind.

Faith rests on the naked Word of God.

When we take Him at His Word,

the heart is at peace.

George Müller

RETURN TO MUMBAI

Six months later, an exciting period of his journey of faith began.

Manoj counted the coins in his pocket. *Not enough to take the bus to the slum*, he knew. In order to evangelize in the different slums, he often had to hike or walk to reach his destination. Sometimes that meant walking a distance of 5 km - one way.

The first step was go around the slum and share the Gospel. While faithfully preaching the word of God, he served the people whom the Lord brought upon his path. Slowly but surely, hearts opened to the message of the Gospel. Families came to faith in Jesus and were discipled. Prayer groups were formed, and the first church was planted.

Together with a team of faithful workers, Manoj continued to sow

Illustrative photo

"Put your ear down to the Bible, and hear Him bid you go and pull sinners out of the fire of sin. Put your ear down to the burdened, agonized heart of humanity, and listen to its pitiful wail for help. Go stand by the gates of hell, and hear the damned entreat you to go to their father's house and bid their brothers and sisters and servants and masters not to come there. Then look Christ in the face — whose mercy you have professed to obey — and tell Him whether you will join heart and soul and body and circumstances in the march to publish His mercy to the world."
William Booth, founder of the Salvation Army

and reap. By God's grace they were able to plant six churches in the slums. Another one was established in Goa state.

Outwardly, the buildings don't look like a church. Between 20-60 people either meet in a house or a rented classroom.

The vision God had given Manoj for Rays of HOPE Ministries was a two-fold vision: "to bring HOPE to hopeless lives by ministering spiritually **and** socially". The spiritual side was already happening: as a result of their mission outreaches, churches had been planted.

"We're not doing much socially," Manoj told his fellow workers. "Once in a while we've been able to help some children, but not as much as I would have liked."

"How can we do more?" someone asked.

"And where to start?" another staff member added. "The needs are so big, and there are so many children."

The team of workers began to pray for God's guidance.

Never satisfied with what he knew, Manoj always wanted to learn new things. As a teenager, he attended the discipleship program of the local church. But he wanted more - a proper Bible education. Manoj longed to attend a three year program on active and practical ministering. However, neither the local church, nor his pastor thought it was a good idea. The main problem was a lack of funds, but in the end, the leadership grudgingly promised to sponsor his studies.

In 1997 he started the residential missiology course, where he was to learn more about missions and theology. However, after being in Bible College for only one month, the church's financial department informed Manoj that no one was willing to sponsor him. The unexpected blow left Manoj with only two options: either to return to Mumbai, or continue on a work scholarship. That year, the young man worked in the garden, cleaned toilets, swept and cleaned the dormitories and classrooms and also studied hard. He became the best student of that college year.

"Lord, what do You want me to do next?" Manoj prayed.
There were no other resources and his church was unwilling to pay for his studies.
Eventually, Manoj realized that it wasn't the degree that mattered. *I have to go back,* he knew.

At the end of the collage year of 1998, Manoj packed his bags to return home.
He looked forward to serve the Lord in Mumbai's mission field.
"I'm going to continue my studies in God's college!" he told his fellow students.

MEETING PINKY

*B*eing an eligible bachelor, Manoj received many marriage proposals.

"It's time you get married!" His family also pressed him.

However, he never had peace about the prospective wife.

In Indian society, it is customary that the younger brother can only marry after the older ones.

"You don't have to wait till I find the right wife," Manoj assured his younger brother. "Please, I want you to get married."

He felt it a privilege to lead his brother's wedding ceremony.

During the year 2000 Manoj was active in different church locations where he met and interacted with many people. It was at a youth gathering that one woman in particular caught his attention. Until that time, the thought of marriage had not been on his agenda – he was too busy doing the Lord's work.

That is the woman of my life, Manoj knew. *She is the one I'm going to marry one day!*

However, during that meeting the two of them never had a chance to speak to each other.

Discreetly, Manoj began to inquire after the woman he had seen. But the more he learned about her, the more discouraged he became.

Pinky, as she was called, and Manoj's family backgrounds were as different as day and night. Coming from a poor family, Manoj was born and raised in a slum. Pinky on the other hand, came from a well-to-do family. Caste wise they were much higher than Manoj, who descended from

> The future is as bright as the promises of God.
>
> William Carey

62

the 'untouchables'. Despite the fact that his family now belonged to the Royal family, to the King of Kings, this didn't change their social status in Indian society.

But that wasn't all. Being in the Lord's service, Manoj had nothing to 'show' for – no savings and no security to provide for his future wife. While pioneering the faith-based ministries of Rays of HOPE. Manoj had to wait upon the Lord to provide. Not only for the ministry, but also for his personal needs. As he did not receive an allowance, he had no financial security to offer.

Pinky, a highly educated woman with a masters degree in commerce, was good looking, light skinned and tall. Manoj, who never went to high school, was short and had a dark skin.
"Humanly speaking, it seems hopeless," Manoj told the Lord. "But I know in my heart that Pinky is Your choice for me, Father." Manoj hoped for an opportunity to talk to her. *I have to find out if she had the same impression,* he thought.
"Lord, if this is from You," Manoj prayed, "If You want us to get married, I know you will work it out. You will make a way for us."

It would take seven years before his prayer was answered and three long years before an opportunity arose in which Manoj could speak privately with the woman who had captivated his heart.

Not knowing how Pinky would react, with trepidation he told her what God had shown him, three years previously.

The beginning of anxiety is the end of faith,
and the beginning of true faith is the end of anxiety.
George Müller

To his amazement, she responded,

"All these years, I have been praying for you too, Manoj. You are the husband God wants for me."

A time of unusual courtship began. Due to family restrictions, Manoj could not meet Pinky in person. Because of the caste differences Pinky's family didn't consent to their daughter's marriage to Manoj. The only way the couple was able to express their love and desire for each other, and to pray together, was over the phone.

Manoj was immersed in the ministry and all the responsibilities that were involved. Pinky worked as an officer at the number one bank of the private sector in Mumbai.
It saddened and hurt the couple that Pinky's family was so opposed to the marriage. Each time Manoj tried to speak with them he was flatly refused.

"You are a beggar," they told him. "You have nothing to offer in the way of a home or finances. How dare you to ask us for Pinky's hand?"
It came as a shock when Manoj found out that not only the local church, but even his own pastor tried to drive him and Pinky apart by talking negatively about him to her family. The couple realized that the enemy also used believers to manipulate the situation. It only strengthened their resolve to trust God to make it happen.
Manoj and Pinky continued to pray over the phone. They also fasted, and beseeched the Lord to change the hearts of her family.

"It is very important we maintain our testimony," Manoj told Pinky. "We are convinced that God wants us to marry, but we should not go against the consent and wishes of your family."

"We will trust and believe that God's timing is perfect," Pinky responded.
With God's grace, they were able to wait patiently for God to answer their prayers.

INDIAN DRESS

Indian clothing throughout history varies widely by region, culture, religion and climate. Saris and the *salwar kameez* - a unisex outfit consisting of loose trousers and a tunic- are traditional attire for Indian women.

Indian men traditionally wear the *lungi, dhoti or kurta*. While European styles frequently appear in large Indian cities like Mumbai, many Indians hold to traditional clothes.

The **sari**, an epitome of Indian culture, is a strip of unstitched cloth, worn by females, ranging from four to nine yards in length that is draped over the body in various styles. It is popular in India and various other countries in the Far East. The most common style is for the sari to

Salwar Kameez

Dhoti

be wrapped around the waist, with one end then draped over the shoulder baring the midriff. The sari is usually worn over a petticoat, with a blouse (*choli* or *ravika*) forming the upper garment. The blouse has short sleeves and a low neck and is usually cropped at the midriff. Cholis, more dressy with plenty of embellishments such as mirrors or embroidery, are often worn on special occasions.

The **dhoti**, also known as **pancha** or **veshti** is the traditional men's garment in India. It is a rectangular piece of unstitched cloth, usually around 4.5 metres long, wrapped around the waist and the legs and knotted at the waist. The Pancha is considered formal wear all over the country and worn to all government and traditional family functions.

GOD ANSWERS PRAYER

*U*ntil his premature death, Pinky's father had been a police-man. In order to support her orphaned family, Pinky's mother, Anita, also joined the police force. Because they lived in the police colony, the family considered themselves high class. There were four girls and one boy who was a sickly child.

Like Manoj's mother had done when he was a baby, Anita too prayed to all the Hindu deities. Visiting the yearly idol festivals, she asked the specific deity to heal her son. But whatever she did, nothing worked and the boy's health didn't improve.

Then one day in 1996, a colleague police woman, shared the gospel with Anita.

"Can I pray for you and your sick child?" the believer asked.

"Yes," Anita replied.

When her shift ended, Anita went home, expecting to find her son weak and sick as usual. She couldn't believe her eyes: her son's condition had improved, and he was even moving around!

Illustrative photo

The miracle of answered prayer opened her heart to the Gospel of Christ. She began to attend a local church and gave up her idol worship.

While Manoj and Pinky steadfastly kept praying for her family, they saw the whole family come to the Lord. God answered their prayers and with it came a change in heart towards Manoj.

"You two can get married," they finally consented.

The same in-laws who used to call Manoj a beggar and treated him with disrespect, became members of his congregation.

He now is respected, and the family admires what God is doing through the couple's lives. Pinky's family is also very supportive of Rays of HOPE Ministry.

Give thanks to the LORD, for he is good; his love endures forever.
Who can proclaim the mighty acts of the LORD
or fully declare his praise?
Blessed are those who act justly, who always do what is right.
Psalm 106:1-3

CHILD LABOUR and STREET CHILDREN

Many parents don't have a choice – their children have to work in order for the family to survive.

Some send their sons to the Zari factories because they cannot afford to look after them. Children from rural areas are sometimes lured to Mumbai by promising them an education, while others are kidnapped.

The 'owners' of these young children often abuse them physically, mentally and sexually. These bonded slaves live miserable lives from which they rarely can escape.

Lately, police have begun to raid these illegal factories. The freed children were brought back to their destitute families, who couldn't look after them in the first place. Until the law against child labour is changed, these raids will only be a recycling of child labour, as many others will take their place.

In order to increase the family's income, many of the hotel boys started working before their 10th birthday. They earn less than Rs. 100 ($ 11) a month, and for that money they often have to work 12 hours a day.

From the age of fifteen, 40% of the girls work as domestic help. They too are often abused: verbally, physically and sexually.

Boys and girls work in local trains, at bus stops, grocery shops, as shoeshine boys, newspaper vendors, waste pickers, hawkers, vendors, babysitters, coolies, etc.

There are more than 100,000 street children in Mumbai who have ended up there either to escape domestic violence, or come from broken families. Sometimes they were neglected. Together with other children they live between the railroad tracks, in house entrances or on the street.

They can't go to school, as it takes all their time and energy just to stay alive. Because they are malnourished, they often suffer from Tuberculosis, malaria, malnutrition and diarrhoea.

2.1 million Indian children die each year before the age of 5.
Four children per minute.

ASHALAYA ~ THE HOUSE OP HOPE

*J*t was early Sunday morning in 1995 that 15 year-old Manoj was on his way to the school building to set things up for the church service. His father had been able to rent a servant's quarter, and they had just moved out of the Ghatkopar slum. It was a big step forward.

Lining the road were large garbage bins where families, restaurants and hotels deposited their leftovers.

How disgusting! Manoj thought when he saw young children searching amongst the filth and eating out of those garbage bins.

He tried to forget those little children but found he couldn't. *Such hopeless eyes,* he thought. *And those hungry looks!* Their dirty faces and skinny bodies began to haunt him.

Street-child eating mango out of the garbage

"Lord, what can be done about this situation?" he prayed.

The answer came by way of another vision: God wanted him to start **ASHALAYA** – the House of HOPE. The fifteen-year-old however, was too young to grasp the daunting task. *How can I ever respond to such enormous need?* Manoj wondered. *Who ARE these children? Where are their parents?*

Manoj was blessed to have both parents. Even though the lower middle class family didn't have any luxury, at least most of the time there was food on the table. Because his parents looked after him, he had clothes to wear and received an elementary education.

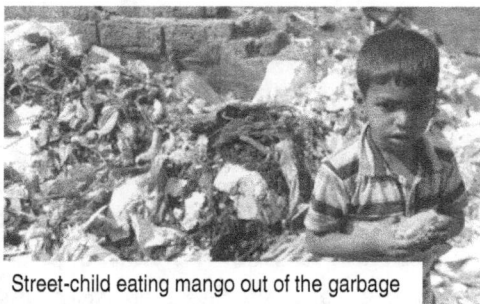

"The children you see roaming the street have lost their parents," someone informed him. "They have no one to care for them."

Manoj tried to imagine their plight. Desperate to survive, these orphans had no choice but to eat out of the garbage.

"Those children have equal rights to live, just like me," Manoj reasoned. "But what can I do?"

From 1995 – 2005, Manoj carried this God-given vision in his heart. Even though he regularly prayed for those orphans, he didn't know when or how he could help them. Where to start?

In 2005, the second phase of Rays of HOPE Ministries began - dealing with the tremendous social needs.

> **Pure and undefiled religion before God and the Father is this: to visit orphans and widows in their trouble, and to keep oneself unspotted from the world.**
> **James 1:27**

According to God's word, it was the responsibility of the body of Christ to care for widows and orphans.

"What are you waiting for?" the Lord challenged Manoj. "Until people start giving you money? Only then are you willing to start? Do you really care and have a heart for these orphans?"

"Yes Lord, I really care." Manoj suddenly knew what to do.

He created a savings box. "When this box is full, we will begin Ashalaya - a house of hope for the orphans," he promised the Lord.

Don't be pulled
by the need,
but by the divine
will of the move
of the Holy
Spirit within you
through God's
word. There are needs everywhere.
They are so big!
He, who comes to a field because of the need,
will be crushed by the need.
But he, who comes with the strength
of the call of God,
Will move through the need and actually fulfill
something of God
to make an impact
on the world
around them.

Randy Smith

2006

Ministering
to the
saints

SERVING A GOD OF MIRACLES

On June 15, 2006, the box was full. It contained Rs. 933 ($ 18). It wasn't much, but he had promised. Manoj knew he had to step out in faith and start the House of Hope. It was time to obey and fulfil the vision God had given him in 1995.

After searching for a suitable place, he found one he thought would fit their needs. However, the owner asked for a Rs. 15,000 ($ 300) security deposit, and a monthly rent of Rs. 3,000 ($ 60). Humanly speaking, he didn't think anyone would be willing to rent out a place to someone who could only pay a deposit of $ 18.

"Lord, You are a God of miracles and wonders!" Manoj began to pray and fast.

During his meeting with the realtor, he shared the vision and the work of Rays of HOPE Ministries.

"It is our desire to establish ASHALAYA the House of HOPE" he said. "We think this house suits our needs."

> Nothing so clears the vision and lifts up the life, as a decision to move forward in what you know to be entirely the will of the Lord.
> John Paton

The realtor's reaction was a direct answer to his prayers.

"Here." The man pressed the key to the apartment in Manoj's hand. "There's no need to pay the deposit and I don't want my commission. You begin to use the place, and pay us the rent at the end of the month."

Through God's wonderful provision the first two orphaned children were to be welcomed in ASHALAYA – the House of HOPE on July 7, 2006.

The 400 sq. feet, one (BHK) ground floor flat contained a small living room, kitchen, one bedroom and one toilet/bathroom.

In order to prepare for the arrival of the children, Manoj went out to buy some groceries.

"I would have loved to invite people for the official opening," he told other believers, "but there is no money to buy snacks or drinks for guests." He thought about the Rs. 933 from the money box. "We need that money to buy food for the children."

At the shop, while debating what to buy, Manoj got a phone call from Pinky. When he stepped outside to talk to her, a shiny black car drove by.

"Manoj!" someone called.

Turning around, Manoj recognized a believer whom he knew dealt in used cars.

"I'm on my way to a business meeting," the man told Manoj. "What are you doing in this part of the city?"

Manoj told him about the House of Hope that was about to open.

"I want to see it!" The man cancelled his meeting and went with Manoj to the home.

The brother asked God to bless the house and prayed for Manoj and his co-workers.

Emptying his pockets before he left, he said, "I'm sorry, but this is all I have with me at the moment."

But to Manoj, those Rs. 300 ($ 6) were a sign from God. It was a longed for and needed confirmation that He was going to provide for their every need.

> Be assured, if you walk with Him and look to Him, and expect help from Him, He will never fail you.
>
> George Müller

74

ASHALAYA's First Home

Because the slum churches pledged to support RHM with Rs. 3,000 per month, somehow Manoj expected that other Christian communities also would be willing to support the work.
But that is not what happened.

Until today, 99% of the donations, in whatever form, come from non-Christians - Hindus, Muslim, people from different walks of life. Each and every time there is a need, help comes from unexpected quarters - just like when Elijah was fed by the ravens.

Whoever destroys a soul,
it is considered
as if he destroyed
an entire world.

And whoever saves a life,
it is considered
as if he saved
an entire world.

Mishnah Sanhedrin 4:5;
Babylonian Talmud
Tractate Sanhedrin 37a

Proud Daddy with his children

ASHALAYA 2007

Reaching out to the street children

Time to do homework

ASHALAYA
2007

God sets the
solitary
in families.
Psalm 68:6

They now have
a place to call
Home
with Food
Clothes
Care and above all
LOVE!

2007, Church service in rented hall

HOPE FOR THE HOPELESS

It was in October 2007 that Pinky's family finally consented for them to get married. The wedding date was set for December 8. During the long years of waiting and trusting God to answer their prayers, both had been saving money for the wedding. In the same period, Rays of HOPE Ministry began to grow and expand.

"I feel God wants us to reach out to the Wadar people," Manoj said one day. The nomadic tribe worked in the stone quarries on the outskirts of Navi Mumbai.

In order to reach this area, Manoj had to pass through Thurbe, the notorious red light district. Not having a motor bike, he was forced to walk 3 km. from the Railway station to reach the slum community. Each time he passed through the red light district, in his heart he condemned the people living and working there.

Look at those whores, Manoj thought. *How can they sell their bodies! Awful!*

He wanted to leave the area as quickly as possible and minister to the Wadar.

CSW waiting for 'clients'

THE WADAR

The Wadar community is one of the many Indian nomadic tribes who are known for their skill as stone-cutters. There are an estimated 300 million Wadar in India.

Due to the wandering traditions over hundreds of years without any ostensible means of livelihood under the influence of the caste system, they are forced to live under sub human conditions.

Society has always looked at them with mistrust and suspicion because of the stigma of criminality attached with them.

In Maharashtra there are three main sub-castes of the Wadars.
1. Mati Wadar (Mati means soil).
2. Jate Wadar (Jate means grinding stone)
3. Gadi Wadar (Gadi means car, vehicle)

Because of the construction boom in urban areas, the demands for Wadar labourers increased. This caused them to settle either on the fringes of the cities near the quarries, or in slums.

Houses given by quarry owners are made of brick or cement blocks, with tin sheets as roofs. Traditional houses have a thatched roof and stick, stone or clay walls. Cooking is usually done in the courtyard.

Around the age of 14, boys join the workforce in the stone quarry. Male adults cut rocks with a sledgehammer. Women sit cross-legged and chip the broken rocks, which are used to build roads. Breaking stones down into small chips is the only work these dark skinned people are allowed to do.

Because of the heavy work, people usually die around the age of 45 to 50. Often their death is caused by an accident in the quarry or because of an illness like tuberculosis, asthma or malaria. Orphaned children stay with relatives. One of the major causes of illness of workers is dust, generated by the breaking and crushing of the stones. Because they cannot pay for doctors and treatment, many suffer and die.

The stone worker family lives near the quarry. After work, they find solace by drinking alcohol. Many smoke or chew a kind of tobacco which invites illness and death.

The parents work from 6 or 7 a.m. till 5 or 6 p.m. Children do the laundry, wash dishes, cook food and look after siblings.
Most of the children look too small and too old for their age. Many suffer from anaemia and malnutrition.

The major Hindu festivals are observed by the Wadars, who also worship ancestral spirits.

A small number of Wadars responded to hearing the Gospel, and have become believers. Many of them cannot read or write, and very little Scripture or other Christian material has been translated into their own language.

Wadar Family

The regular visits of the outreach team to the Wadar slum began to bear fruit. There was joy in heaven and on earth, when Rays of HOPE Ministries was able to plant a church there.

Women's meeting in Wadar slum

"And what about those people living in the Thurbe district?" the Lord challenged Manoj.
God opened his eyes to the desperate needs of that dark neighbourhood.

"We too have this burden," the outreach team responded. "We have to do something to help these people."
When believers began to pray for ways to do outreach and share the Gospel in Thurbe, Manoj was reminded of the story of Jesus and the woman caught in adultery. The Lord didn't say anything, just kept writing in the sand. Eventually, no one was left to accuse the woman. With compassion, Jesus didn't condemn or reject her. Instead, He blessed her, by saying, "Go in peace, but sin no more!"

Prostitution and CSWE

In India, it is legal to exchange sexual services for money. However, it is illegal to solicit in a public place, keep a brothel, to pimp or pander.

Female prostitutes can be:
- Common prostitutes
- Singers and dancers
- Call girls
- Religious prostitutes (Devadasi)
- or so-called caged brothel prostitutes.

"For those entering Thurbe, there is no way out. It is a dead end."

Human trafficker

Mumbai's oldest Red Light District used to be situated in Kamatipura, on Grand Road E. The development of an affluent residential colony forced the CSW to move to a new district. They relocated to Indira Nagar, the industrial area of Thurbe, in Navi Mumbai.

The women work and live in cramped rooms with dingy tiled walls. Through filthy passages people are smuggled through the ceiling. Annually, more than 300 girls between 12 and 16 years old are reported missing. Most end up in Thurbe, never to be heard of again.

CSEW (Commercially Sexually Exploited Women) are pushed into the trade at a young age, often before puberty. They can be as young as twelve years old and don't leave until the brothel keeper has earned enough money through them. Because most of the girls do not receive any education, they have no idea how much they earn. It is a vicious circle from which it is very difficult to break free.

Young girl, being prepared to enter the 'business'

83

When a woman or girl refuses to obey the demands of the pimp, she is physically and mentally tortured.

The number of prostitutes has doubled in the last decade, also because there is an increase in sex tourism. Human Rights Watch estimates that there are more than 200,000 sex workers in Mumbai, the biggest number in Asia.

Women are only allowed to leave when they become ill, often because they have AIDS. Having no place to go, these women end up on the street.

Nowadays, several government organizations try to create awareness about HIV and AIDS. Many non-profit organizations working in the Red Light District have independent and specific goals. This can be health, education, or overall rehabilitation of the women and their children.

HOPE Center takes care of the children of CSW and provides full-time care, protection and education through a day and night shelter in a residential home, away from the Red Light district.

Children of Sex workers

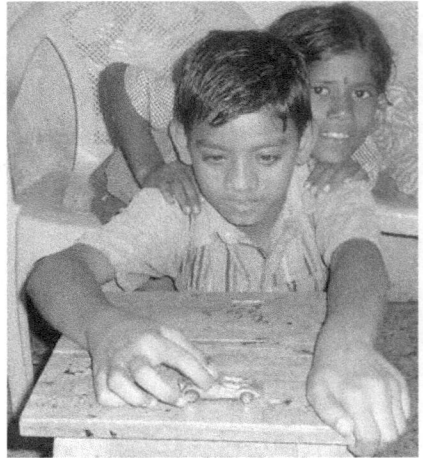

HOPE CENTER

What moved Manoj most was the plight of the children growing up in the red light district. Day and night they were bombarded with sexual immorality and nobody seemed concerned about them. These tragic children couldn't help it that they were born out of prostitution. Their mothers didn't want them, and there were no fathers to claim them. At night, the child had to watch his or her mother having sexual relationships with one customer after another. When the child was very young, the mother often gave him drugs or liquor, anything to keep him sleeping under the bed. She could not be interrupted while 'working'.

"What will their future be like?" Manoj wondered as he watched the malnourished, neglected children, none of whom went to school. "This evil manipulates and badly influences their young minds." The knowledge angered him. "Why are they robbed of their innocence and their future?"

In ASHALAYA, TV programmes were monitored and their children lived sheltered lives. For the children of sex workers, immorality was a 'normal' way of life.

Most of the women working in Thurbe, Mumbai's main red light district, had been sold into prostitution. Often, this had been under false promises of marriage.

However, it was also possible that, because of extreme poverty, the family sold their daughter into prostitution.

Many times, orphaned girls were sold by their relatives.
Others were deceived and trapped by people involved in sex rackets. Most women, whether single or widows, worked in groups under a pimp, or under a madam. Many of them were 2nd generation prostitutes. What other way did they have to earn their income? They never learned another trade, and even if they did, society would never accept them.

A big city like Mumbai attracted many migrants looking for work. They left their wives and families behind in the rural areas. Those who wanted to satisfy their fleshly cravings, flocked to Thurbe.

After lots of prayer, the team of Rays of HOPE Ministries knew God also wanted them to begin their outreach in the red light district. The vision for "HOPE Centre" was born.

"If we start this ministry," a team member said, "we're going to need a building."

"Lord, please guide us to the right place," the believers prayed. "May it bring light and hope in this dark area."

FOR RENT the sign said.
The premises seemed ideal for the purpose – a place to minister to the children of sex workers. Through them, they also hoped to reach out to the mothers.
Manoj met with the owner of the place, who agreed to rent it out to them. He wanted a Rs. 30,000 ($ 600) security deposit, and a monthly rent of Rs. 2,200 ($ 45).

"We would like to rent it," Manoj told the owner.

It was a step of faith, for the ministry didn't have any money.
As they always did, Manoj and his co-workers began to pray about the situation. Of course he also shared the problem with Pinky.
She too began to pray for the HOPE Centre-to-be.

"Why don't we use the money we saved for our wedding?" Pinky suggested. "We can sow what God has given us into the HOPE Center."

With one accord, the couple desired to give up their savings.

> God judges what we give by what we keep.
>
> George Müller

"With this money, we can save the lives of many children," Manoj said. To them, it was a joyful sacrifice. The Rs. 28,000 ($ 580) of their savings account was used to rent the HOPE Center, which began on October 15, 2007.

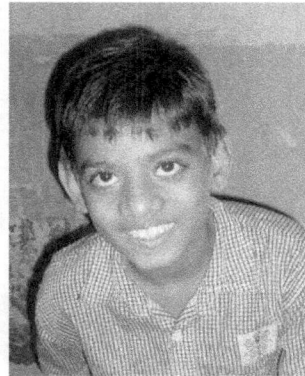

> Whoever oppresses the poor shows contempt for their Maker, but whoever is kind to the needy honours God.

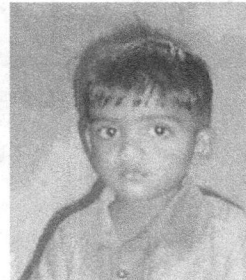

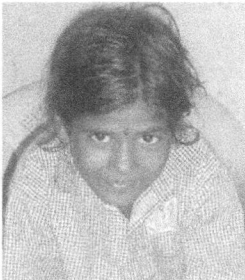

THE WEDDING

God honours sacrificial giving. One week after having invested in the Heavenly Kingdom, the Lord began to provide for Manoj and Pinky's personal needs.

It was Sunday morning, and Manoj welcomed the people arriving at the slum church. A believer handed Manoj an envelope.

"Where would you like us to use it for?" Manoj asked her. "The orphanage or the church?"

Smiling, the woman shook her head. "No, this money is for your wedding."

Manoj knew she made her living by collecting scrap material from the street and garbage belts. By selling used items to dealers, she earned about $ 2 a day. It was the only way she could provide for her family.

Manoj and Pinky were touched by her gift of Rs. 1,800 (about $ 45) for their wedding. It was the first donation of many that followed.

They never had to ask for money. Neither did they have to contract a loan to pay for the wedding expenses. The Lord provided for all their needs.

Manoj and Pinky's wedding on December 8, 2007 was attended by over 1,000 guests!

"From now on, I will not call you Pinky any more," Manoj told his radiant bride. "You will be called "Priya" — beloved."

88

Be assured, if you walk with Him
and look to Him
and expect help from Him,
He will never fail you.

George Müller

89   ASHALAYA'S children at the wedding

The married couple moved in with Manoj's parents, who now lived in Kula, in East Mumbai. Both of his brothers and their families had their own apartments.

Tukaram and Muktabai's house was a 250 sq. feet flat which contained a living room, kitchen and a toilet/bathroom. Because it had no bedroom, in the evening the tiny kitchen became the bedroom of the newly-weds.

Manoj desired for his wife to become actively involved in the ministry and be part of all that was happening. That was impossible if Priya continued to work full-time in a secular job. Manoj didn't want to ask his wife to quit her well-paying job. Unable to give her a life of luxury from the small allowance he received, he would feel guilty. Manoj desired to live in dignity, and not give people the impression that he lived on his wife's salary.

It had become a trend for Christian pastors and evangelists to marry either nurses or graduated, working women. Because they had become the breadwinners of the family, these women no longer respected their husbands. Also church members criticised those pastors and evangelists. "That lazy pastor lives well because his wives works."

Manoj wanted to take responsibility and care for his wife, family and children to come. He longed to support her by faith, not based on the security of a fixed salary. Manoj desired to serve God with his beloved - shoulder to shoulder and hand in hand.

Unable to ask his wife to quit her job, he prayed.

And God spoke to Priya's heart - she resigned from her well-paying job.

"We will trust You for our needs, Lord," Manoj prayed. "From now on, the two of us will serve you full-time."

OPEN DOORS

When team members of Rays of HOPE Ministries began their outreach in Thurbe, they encountered opposition and closed hearts. Most prostitutes refused to talk to the female team members; they didn't want to invite them in, let alone send their children to HOPE Center.

Despite the fact that the mothers refused to send their children, the team continued to pray and work with them.
Slowly, the dedication, humbleness and faithfulness of the team members began to bear fruit. Thurbe's inhabitants couldn't help but notice God's love in action. Their hearts began to soften, especially when they saw the changes for good in the lives of their children.

Women began to express their appreciation for the work of the team, and treated them with high regard. Eight children from the Red Light district now have a home in ASHALAYA.

In the middle of this dark corner of Navi Mumbai, HOPE Center became a beacon of God's light and hope.

Nowadays, everyone knows about HOPE Center's activities.

From Monday to Saturday, the Center is open from 9 a.m. till 4 p.m. Team members arrive around 9 a.m. and first have devotions together. The premises are then prepared for the arrival of the children. Around 9.30 a.m. the 3-8 eight-year-olds are warmly welcomed for kindergarten. Their program is 10 a.m. until 12.30 p.m. At 1 p.m. children of all ages receive a nutritious meal, prepared by the staff. Each day there is a different menu, of which the main part consists of rice, bread and curry. This is combined with either vegetables, eggs or chicken.

Because of limited resources, HOPE Center can only provide a daily lunch for the 100+ children aged 3-16 .

The ministry would also love to provide dinner for them, but lack the funds to do so.

Feeding the mind
Learning means empowerment

Feeding the body
to keep it healthy and strong

Feeding the heart
Playing games and having fun

Feeding the soul
Learning about their Heavenly
Father who loves them.

Each child is welcomed and accepted, even if he has lice, is dirty and unwashed. These children are loved as they are - which is a novelty to them.

Staff members try to educate and teach the children how to take care of themselves. "You are God's child," they tell them, "so you have to learn to stay neat and clean."

Most of the activities are geared towards the children. They attend school from Monday to Friday and take part in the daily feeding program.

Saturday's Junior Church or 'children's club' is also open to all.

On Thursday afternoon the Center is open for the mothers. Everyone is invited to come to the prayer meeting.
A few women have begun to come. They listen to God's word, receive counselling and when requested, a female staff member prays for and with the prostitute.

HOPE Center is run by dedicated and committed team members. Because the ministry cannot afford full-time workers, one of Ashalaya's female caretakers and one of the Home's older girls work together with believers from the church. As a team, they serve the needy in Thurbe.
Whenever she can Priya, too, is actively involved in this project; Manoj visits the project every other day. None of the staff members receive a salary, only a small allowance.

HOPE Centre Thurbe

Reaching out to lost souls and....

...Welcoming them into the Kingdom of God

ASHALAYA celebration

2008

"Why are you absent when I need you the most?"

*A*shalaya's house began to burst at the seams.
What had started out with two children had grown to seventeen. Together with the five caretakers this meant twenty-two people had to share a small 400 sq. feet house with one toilet and bathroom. Children could only sleep in one position - it was impossible to turn around once they were settled in for the night.
Neighbouring apartments began to complain about the noise, and the children were not allowed to play outside.

"We don't want those beggars living here!" a neighbour said.

"Those bastards have to leave!" another added.

The staff of Rays of HOPE Ministries prayed, "Lord, we need a bigger and better place!"
Manoj began searching for a suitable home for his growing ASHA-LAYA family.

No room to turn around during the night!

Even though Manoj and Priya loved ASHALAYA'S precious children, who called them "Daddy" and "Mama", they also longed to have their own babies.

How thrilled and grateful they were when God answered their prayers and Priya expected their first child. It was a sad day when she lost the baby after seven weeks of pregnancy. The couple struggled with their personal loss and heartache.

They were hopeful when Priya was expecting again. But for no obvious reason, she lost the baby again after seven weeks.

"Why, Lord?" they cried.

Manoj struggled with the loss and felt spiritually low.

"Lord, I'm preaching and believing You are a God of miracles," he complained. "So why do we have to suffer this loss - twice?"

He didn't feel like going out and ministering to others in need. The servant of God himself needed to be comforted and encouraged. He longed for a sign from heaven, telling him what to do next.

Knowing about Manoj's emotional struggle, a friend called him.

"I'm on my way to a seminar," he said. "I think you should come with me."

"I don't feel like going." Manoj wanted to stay home and mourn his loss.

It took a lot of persuasion, but eventually Manoj reluctantly joined his friend.

Learning about the topic of the seminar, he held his breath: **"Why are you absent when I need you the most?"**

Sitting next to Manoj was a young man. They only exchanged smiles and business cards. "Benjamin" the card said.

That evening, many of Manoj's unspoken questions were answered. His heavy heart felt much lighter, and he sensed a relief in spirit. God knew exactly what he needed most.

After a six month search, Manoj found the right place for his ASHALAYA family. The house was free standing. It had a 100 sq. meter ground floor plus second story of 2200 sq. feet. However, the owner wanted Rs. 8,000 ($ 200) per month and a security deposit of Rs. 100,000 ($ 2,000).

"You have one day to decide," the realtor told Manoj that Friday evening. "I must have your answer before Saturday evening at 8.30 p.m."

Early Saturday morning Manoj contacted the man who was responsible for the finances of Rays of HOPE Ministries.

"How much do we have in the ministry account?" he asked with trepidation.

"We have Rs. 46,000 ($ 1,000) in the ministry and church account," the believer replied.

Together with Priya he prayed about what to do next and both felt they had to use their savings in order to secure the rent. This brought the sum to Rs. 74,000.

Manoj's heart fell. "That means we have to come up with another Rs. 26,000 ($ 600)!" [At that time, the dollar rate was much higher.]

Facing an emergency situation, there was only one more thing the couple could do now.

"We have to sell our jewellery." Priya voiced what he also felt they should do.

"The shop opens at 11 a.m.," Manoj said. "Then I will sell our wedding rings, and your locket. I hope it will be enough."

At 9.30 a.m. the phone rang.

"This is Benjamin," the caller introduced himself. "We met last month, during the seminar. Do you remember me?"
Manoj did, but vaguely.

"I'd like to come and visit you, and to see the orphanage," Benjamin said.

"I'm sorry, but today is not a good day," Manoj said. "I'm in a hurry and have to go to a shop."

"It will only be for five minutes," Benjamin pressed. "I just have to see you."

"All right," Manoj consented. "You can come to my parent's house." He gave him directions how to get there.

At 10.30 a.m. Benjamin stood on their doorstep.
After exchanging some pleasantries, he handed Manoj a light envelope.

"God has been constantly speaking to my heart," he explained. "He wants me to help your ministry. This is the first pay-check I received for my work in Mumbai."

Manoj's heart skipped a beat when he saw the cheque. It was Rs. 26,700 (more than $ 600) - the biggest donation the ministry had ever received. And, it was even more than the money they needed at that particular moment!

The Lord had been testing their faith. In the end there was no need to sell their wedding jewellery. God provided the money that was needed to secure the lease for ASHALAYA's new home.

> Everyone was amazed and gave praise to God.
> They were filled with awe and said,
> "We have seen remarkable things today."
> Luke 5:26

GOD PROVIDES

Ashalaya's children needed milk for their calcium intake and nutrition. However, milk was expensive - Manoj couldn't even afford to buy 1/2 - 1 litre per day. And that wasn't even enough for morning tea.

One day, Manoj was in the dairy shop when he noticed that the shop owner kept staring at him. *What does he want from me?* Manoj thought.

Finally, the man came over. "Who are you?" he wanted to know. "And what are you doing? I see you with all these children."

Manoj told him the story of Ashalaya.

The diary shop owner was noticeably touched. "Where do you live?"

Manoj gave him the address.

"Tomorrow, I will send someone to deliver 5 litres of milk," the man promised.

Manoj hesitated. *What if he charges me for the milk?* he wondered.

"Thank you kindly, sir. But can we perhaps get the milk at a discount?"

"Forget about paying!" the man exclaimed. "This is my contribution to you, for your work!"

Until this very day, this Hindu dairy shop owner has been delivering free milk for Ashalaya's growing family each and every day.

> Let us see that we keep God before our eyes;
> that we walk in His ways and seek to please and glorify
> Him in everything, great and small. Depend upon it, God's
> work, done in God's way, will never lack God's supplies.
> Hudson Taylor

ASHALAYA
2009

Their daily glass of milk

Outreach

2009

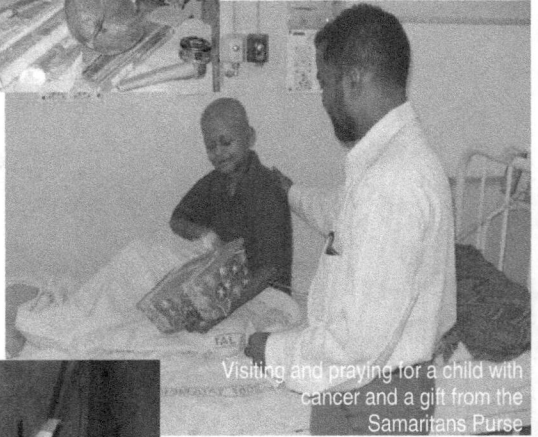
Visiting and praying for a child with cancer and a gift from the Samaritans Purse

2009 independence day celebrations at HOPE Center

SOWING AND REAPING
IN THURBE

*A*fter four years of faithfully working in Thurbe, the people, the pimps and the families living there knew the believers could be trusted, and only had their welfare in mind. No longer were the team members in danger when they entered the district. By God's grace, they were welcomed with appreciation and respect.

It was an answer to prayer when more women began to attend the prayer meetings in the HOPE Centre.

"But what do we do when a woman wants to stop working as a Commercial Sex Worker?" a team member asked. "How can we help them?"

"Even if she wants out of this bondage," another worker added, "the woman first has to pay off her debts."

"Debts?"

"Yes, because she was sold into prostitution and the pimp or sex racketeer bought her for a high price," the worker explained. "Most women don't know how much they earn, and the pimp won't tell her."

In recent years, many Commercial Sex Workers had been rescued by an agency run by Indian Social workers.
However, due to the lack of a solid rehabilitation program, most rescued women returned to prostitution. Society refused to accept ex-CSW's, who often didn't have a family to return to.
Without an education, they had no other way to earn money for their daily needs. The helpless, destitute woman was forced to go back to prostitution - the only 'trade' she knew.

Rays of HOPE Ministries longed to provide a place of refuge to shelter these trapped women. Those willing to be rescued, had to be rehabilitated through a solid program. By taking them out of their environment they would be able to have a better life and a brighter future.

"How can we, as believers, help them, Lord?" the team prayed. "And where can we create this place of refuge?"

A CITY OF HOPE
The Vision is Born

God used Manoj to pioneer the Rays of HOPE Ministries, and gradually more believers had been added to the team. The faithful staff members faced many challenges. The ministry now looked after the needs of orphans, widows, the destitute, the sexually abused, those trapped into prostitution, the children of sex workers and HIV patients. Daily, they came into contact with and who were struggling with hopeless situations.

In 2009, the Lord gave Manoj a dream. *You are to build a City of HOPE*, God told him.
After praying about this vision for some time, Manoj shared this idea with fellow believers and several pastors to whom he was accountable.

"We feel that such a city is God's will," they told him.
"Thank you, Lord, for this confirmation," Manoj said.

Gradually, the outline for this City of HOPE began to take shape.
It was to be one campus - a closed community - that would function as a place of refuge for whoever faced a hopeless situation.

104

The City of Hope would shelter HIV infected children, and have a rehabilitation home for prostitutes and their children who wanted to leave their lives of bondage. It would offer literacy courses and occupational training in order to help ex-prostitutes to become self-reliant and empowered.

There would be a home for widows, who could participate and be involved with the other activities; these women could have their own share in the work. In this haven, deprived old people, with no one to look after them, could die in peace and with dignity. In the terminal care centre those dying of HIV/AIDS would be looked after.
A prayer centre would be a place to worship God, listen to His Word, be blessed, transformed, receive prayer, healing and deliverance.

The Bible School on the premises would teach new believers how to follow and serve the Lord through evangelism and missions.

Many ASHALAYA-type family units would be spread out over the compound. Here, eight orphaned children would live as a family, led by a Godly couple, perhaps with their own children. This would ensure that each child would receive proper care, love, attention and discipline.

Sheltered in the City of HOPE, wounded souls would find love and respect from the community living there.
Staff members could minister to people's spiritual needs and pray for them; they would be available to help those dealing with emotional issues, and ask God for spiritual deliverance.

The practical needs for this big mission and grand undertaking seem enormous, but the staff know they serve a mighty God!

"I believe that the City of HOPE is going to be a powerful way of God's work in the lives of people living there," one of the staff workers said.

"And at same time, it will show Christ in action to the world around us," another believer added.

The beginning of Project ASHA

While ministering to the needy, Manoj and his fellow workers often came in contact with HIV infected people. First-hand they saw how AIDS affected and changed the lives of everyone involved - the AIDS sufferer, his or her family and everyone around them.

ABOUT HIV AND AIDS

In short: HIV is a virus while AIDS is a definition.
HIV = Human Immunodeficiency Virus
AIDS = Acquired Immune Deficiency Syndrome.
This is a group of symptoms and diseases associated with the damage HIV does to the immune system. An ongoing HIV infection damages the immune defence cells, thus the body is less able to fight off infection. E.g. for an HIV positive person chickenpox can be fatal.

An HIV positive person can look and feel healthy. It may be years before people know they are infected. However, the carriers are infecting others through blood, semen, vaginal fluid and breast milk. Gradually, the HIV positive person becomes sicker and sicker, and develops AIDS.
HIV is NOT spread through air, food, water, insects or toilet seats. Therefore, patients don't need to use separate dishes or cutlery.

Difference between AIDS and HIV positive
A person has AIDS when the numbers of specific types of cells in their immune system drop below a certain level. Or when they develop one of a specific group of opportunistic infections.
An **opportunistic infection** is an infection by a micro organism that nor-

mally does not cause disease but becomes pathogenic when the body's immune system is impaired and unable to fight off infection.

H - Human: because this virus can only infect human beings.
I - Immune-deficiency: because the effect of the virus is to create a deficiency, a failure to work properly, within the body's immune system.
V - Virus: one of the characteristics of a virus is that it is incapable of reproducing by itself. However, it takes over the machinery of the human cell.

A - Acquired: this condition is not transmitted through the genes but has to be acquired or be infected with.
I - Immune: the body's immune system is affected, which usually works to fight off bacteria and viruses.
D - Deficiency: because it makes the immune system deficient (not work properly)
S - Syndrome: someone with AIDS may experience a wide range of different diseases and opportunistic infections.

Unborn babies can be infected with HIV, or get the virus from their mother's breast milk. AIDS children need the same things as healthy children – lots of love and affection. Because they are prone to germs and infections, special care must be taken. E.g. they cannot play in sand boxes which were used by animals as a litter box. Stuffed and furry toys need to be washed regularly. Normal childhood infections, like chickenpox, can be fatal for children who are HIV positive or already have AIDS.

> "Women don't only bear the burden of HIV infection, they also bear the burden of HIV care. Grandmothers are looking after their children. Women are caring for their dying husbands. Children are looking after dying parents and surviving siblings." Nelson Mandela.

DAIWIK'S STORY

*A*fter faithfully reaching out and sowing into the Wadar community, God answered the prayers of the believers. He gave them a harvest of redeemed souls - people accepted Jesus as their Saviour and Lord.

Daiwik (means by the Grace of God - not his real name) was a middle-aged stone mason who offered to help the team build a small church in the slum. Manoj had the joy of leading this Wadar man to the Lord. Daiwik and his family began to attend the services. No one knew the reason why they suddenly stopped coming to church.

"I'm going to talk to Daiwik." Manoj went over to their house. It was empty.

"Where is Daiwik and his family?" he asked a neighbour.

"They left." The woman shrugged. "Don't know where they went."

It seemed that Daiwik had disappeared without leaving a trace.

Years went by without any news of Daiwik and his family.

Then one day in 2012, the Lord reminded Manoj of this Wadar stone mason. Burdened, he began to pray for Daiwik and renewed his search for him.

He had no address. The only information he obtained was a vague indication of a certain place. Led by the Lord, Manoj managed to locate Daiwik. Approaching the building, he saw a man who looked like a walking skeleton.

"Daiwik?" Manoj was shocked when he realised it was the same man who used to be strong and healthy.

"Manoj!" Daiwik cried out when he recognized him. Hugging him tight, he burst into tears.

Too weak to stand, Daiwik sat down on the pavement. Sitting next to him, Manoj listened to Daiwik's heart wrenching story.

"When my wife and children learned that I was HIV positive, everyone looked down on me." He let out a shivering sigh. "Not only that, they stopped talking to me."

"Why are you outside the house?" Manoj wanted to know.

"When my health deteriorated, they didn't want me living with them any more." Daiwik pointed to a narrow place between the wall and a drainage gutter filled with sewage. "That's where I live now. When it rains, I cover myself with a sheet of plastic."

"But what about your food?" Manoj's heart went out to this hopeless, rejected man.

"They scrape it from their plate onto mine, making sure they don't touch anything." He began to cry bitterly.

That day Manoj learned first-hand about the stigma, rejection and separation AIDS causes. Looking at Daiwik's pain, he knew that the physical hardships caused by AIDS were more bearable than the agony of rejection. His wife and children, whom he loved, worked and cared for all of his life, had been treating him worse than a rabid dog.

Putting his arm around Daiwik, Manoj began to pray for him. Counselling the hopeless, dying man, he encouraged him to return to the Lord. "You may have forgotten the Lord, but God has not forgotten you, my brother!"

Daiwik asked God's forgiveness and gave his miserable life back to the Lord.

"Have you heard?" a staff member asked Manoj a week later. "They found Daiwik's dead body on the road side."

"You know what happened?" Manoj was grateful he had been able to pray with the dying man.

"We don't know, but when they notified his wife and children of Daiwik's death, they refused to have the body brought home."

The man shook his head in unbelief. "Instead, they ordered it to be taken away and cremated. "

"The stigma of HIV and AIDS can only be removed by awareness campaigns," Manoj later told his fellow workers. "As believers, we should be involved in this important aspect of educating the people."

Project ASHA was added to the Rays of HOPE Ministries.
Believers who are willing to become involved in this ministry undergo professional health training and education. By partnering with another organisation for health-care education and training purposes, ASHA now ministers to a few families.

Team members learn that the most important part of educating the people is to explain what HIV and AIDS is and isn't, and how it can be prevented. The staff worker talks to the family about the importance of moral values and of commitment and fidelity to their spouse. While counselling and encouraging these distraught families, they stress the importance of family members caring for the HIV/AIDS sufferer.

Through leaflets, announcements, private conversations and group meetings, ASHA now caters to all segments of the Indian society - from prostitutes and slum dwellers to higher cast families.

Mr. and Mrs. Sanjay, both HIV-positive, are helped through Project ASHA

DIGNITY and EMPOWERMENT

*P*roject **Dignity**, which began in 2008, is today still considered to be in the 'baby phase'. Because there are no designated funds and resources available, Rays of HOPE Ministries can only help a few widows and children each year.

Sponsoring Widows

An Indian family is dependant on the man of the household. Women suffer when a husband dies, even when there are grown children. Often, married children have their own lives and families to take care of, and they don't want the additional burden of having to care for their widowed mother.

Especially young widows face an uncertain and bleak future. As house wives, they always depended on the husband's income. Lacking higher education, the woman doesn't know how to provide for her children. In order to survive, these women often end up in prostitution. It is either that, or starve.

By May 2012, the project has sponsored six widows over 50 years of age, who lived below the poverty line. Most of them come from non-Christian backgrounds, but through the project have become believers in Christ. Regardless of religious background or caste, widows who are in great need, and fit the criteria, will be sponsored.

Mrs. Pakiam

The **SCHOLARSHIP FUND** tries to help children regardless of caste or religion. These children do have families, but their parents are too poor to pay for further education. Children who are of post-primary, intermediate and high school age are assisted by providing them with books, notebooks and exercise books.

It is the hope and prayer of Rays of HOPE Ministries to help more children. This is only possible when more donations are given towards the Scholarship fund.

Presently, Rays of HOPE Ministries has a **SEWING UNIT**, but the team is praying for an expansion of this important tool to empower widowed and underprivileged women. More machines means more women can be trained and taught specific skills to make clothes. By selling them locally, this will give them steady employment.

MICRO BUSINESS LOAN PROJECT

In order to overcome poverty, one needs to be self-reliant. In order to help people come out of the cycle of poverty, Rays of HOPE Ministries can offer a small business loan. This plays an important role in starting a business. With the Lord's blessings and proper guidance these people have a future and a hope.

Mr. Ashok's transport business is up and running

Mrs. Sindhubai selling her vegetables

Dignity & Empowerment

Ravi Shinde selling dried fish

Give us this day our daily bread...

*P*arents are expected to prepare proper wheat bread and vegetables for their children to eat during school recess. Snacks, biscuits or junk-food are not allowed.

Every morning, the believers working in ASHALAYA's kitchen bake fresh wheat bread for the children to take to school.

Indian staple food

One day, the women informed Manoj, "There is no more wheat flour to bake bread tomorrow morning."

Facing a real problem, as there was no money to buy wheat flour, Manoj said, "We better start praying!"

Around 5 p.m. that afternoon, a group of Hindu ladies, who worshiped a particular idol, came by.

"For a long time we have been looking for you," one of them said. "We heard about ASHALAYA, and wanted to help you, but couldn't find the Home."

"Can you please tell us how we can help?" another Hindu lady asked.

"What do you need most?" A woman pointed to a heavy bag. "Can you perhaps use this?" The bag contained 50 kg of wheat flour.

"We would like to donate this on a regular, monthly basis," one of the ladies said.

"Thank you very much!" Manoj was overwhelmed with joy.

Over the last three years, every second day of the month, these Hindu ladies have been faithfully donating wheat flour. Without fail they continue to bless the children of ASHALAYA.

MARATHI is an Indo-Aryan language spoken by the Marathi people of western and central India. Marathi has some of the oldest literature of all modern Indo-Aryan languages, dating from about 1000 AD. It is the official language of the Indian state of Maharashtra and spoken in India by 64,783,000 people.

Business in the municipal corporation is also transacted in Marathi. On the streets Mumbaiya (Bambaiya) Hindi is spoken. This is a blend of Hindi, Urdu and Marathi with some invented colloquial words. English is the working language of the city's white collar workforce.

THE BIBLE IN MARATHI

Part of the Bible was published for the first time in 1807.

The New Testament was first published in 1811.

The complete Bible was first published in 1821.

Picture: first verses from the Gospel of John, 1994 version, published by The Bible Society of India, Bangalore.

योहानकृत शुभवर्तमान

१ प्रारंभी शब्द होता, आणि शब्द देवासह होता आणि शब्द देव होता. २ तोच प्रारंभी देवासह होता. ३ सर्व कांहीं त्याच्याद्वारें झालें आणि जें कांहीं झालें तें त्याच्याबांचून झालें नाहीं. ४ त्याच्या ठायीं जीवन होतें, व तें जीवन मनुष्य- मात्राचा प्रकाश होतें. ५ तो प्रकाश अंधारांत प्रकाशतो; तरी अंधारानें त्याला ग्रासलें नाहीं.

६ देवानें पाठविलेला एक मनुष्य प्रगट झाला; त्याचें नाव योहान. ७ तो साक्षीकरितां म्हणजे त्या प्रकाशाविषयीं साक्ष देण्याकरितां आला; ह्यासाठीं कीं, त्याच्याद्वारें सर्वांनीं विश्वास ठेवावा. ८ हा तो प्रकाश नव्हता, तर त्या प्रकाशाविषयीं साक्ष देण्याकरितां आला.

NAVI MUMBAI is the largest planned city on the planet, with a total area of 344 square kilometres (133 sq mi). It was developed in 1972 and has a population of about 2,6000,000. It lies on the mainland on the eastern shore of Thane Creek and is connected by the Vashi and Airoli Bridges.

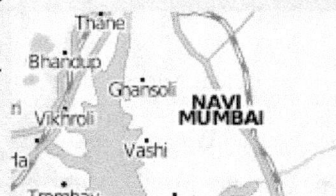

Navi Mumbai International Airport is expected to open in 2014.

Certain areas of the hilly region are protected wetlands.
Navi Mumbai is a cosmopolitan city – the majority of the population is Hindu (86%), Muslims (10%). Also Christians and Sikhs live in Navi Mumbai.

KHARGAR HILLS (Belapur) is a lush green mountain area - a favourite place for Mumbaikars to walk, picnic, enjoy nature and the scenery. When the rains begin, many come to the area to see the Pandavakhada waterfall.

CARE HOME

*T*he vision for CARE HOME came in 2009 when Manoj met an eight-year-old critically ill boy. Sajan (beloved - not his real name) lay on the roadside. Manoj held his water bottle to the cracked lips. Sajan drank thirstily, only to vomit the precious liquid out again. Diarrhoea had weakened the malnourished child even more.

"Where are your parents?" Manoj asked the dying child.

"Dead. AIDS," Sajan whispered. "When I was about three or four years old."

"Did you live with relatives?" Manoj already guessed what came next.

"Till I was five," the boy was almost too weak to talk. "Then they threw me out."

Probably because he was HIV positive, Manoj thought. "Where did you live then?" His heart went out to the child.

"On the streets. Begging."

Sajan didn't have to say more - Manoj knew the scenario: Because of malnutrition and AIDS, Sajan's health rapidly deteriorated. However, what eventually killed him wasn't the starvation, but the rejection and utter loneliness the child experienced.

"I don't know what's wrong with me!" Sajan cried bitterly. "I remember my papa. When I cried he'd pick me up and buy me a candy to make me smile." His voice broke. "Today, I'm crying so much, but nobody wants to come near me. No one wants to touch me." His desperate eyes looked at Manoj. "What's wrong with me?" he wailed.

Manoj's felt utterly helpless. *I can't help this precious child because it is already too late. He is dying!*

Worse than dying of starvation had been the loneliness and rejection.

This heartbreaking experience was the birth of the CARE HOME. The house was to be a haven for children like Sajan.

In the last decade, more and more people have become HIV positive. Many parents are dying of AIDS. India struggles with the largest number of AIDS-orphans in the world, and their number is growing each day.

The staff of Rays of HOPE Ministries feels the responsibility to try and shelter as many of these innocent victims as possible.

By July 2012, CARE HOME looks after five HIV infected, orphaned children. The health of the oldest girl is slowly deteriorating, and presently she shows more AIDS symptoms.

CARE HOME staff, none of whom have a medical background, don't receive a salary, only a small allowance. Once a month the children have a check-up, undergo a blood test and receive their quota of NRTI's (nucleoside reverse transcriptase inhibitors - a class of HIV medication- anti viral drugs). This medication prolongs their life span. While NRTI treatment is provided for free by the Indian government, Rays of HOPE ministries pays for the rest of the necessary treatments.

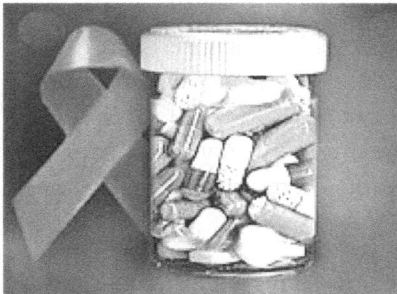

It has become obvious to the staff that CARE HOME needs their own place. Until another solution is found, one room in Ashalaya is used for this purpose.

A sick child, too weak to participate, lies on the floor during prayer time.

HIV infected children tire quickly, they have specific needs and require more care than the other (healthy) children in the home.

It is the prayer of the CARE HOME staff that the children under their care stay 'healthy', for as long as the Lord gives them the grace to live. They realize that that, unless the Lord miraculously heals them, the HIV infected children of CARE HOME are going to die of AIDS. But they will die knowing they are cared for till the very end.

And most important of all - these children know they are loved.

There are three stages in the work of God:

1. Impossible
2. Difficult
3. Done

Hudson Taylor

Preaching the Gospel at the beach

ASHALAYA outing to a WaterPark

2010

TRAVELLING THE WORLD

*I*n 2008, an Australian couple, Amanda and Darren, volunteered at ASHALAYA for a few weeks. "Why don't you come and visit us in Australia?" they invited Manoj.
It wasn't until the beginning of 2010 that Manoj was able to come to Brisbane, Australia, for an extended visit. Well prepared with brochures and ideas on how to raise money for Rays of HOPE ministries, just before landing God spoke to his heart that he was NOT to ask for money. *You are to give, share what I put on your heart, and minister spiritually to the people you are going to meet,* the Lord told him.

For 25 days, Manoj spoke and met with individuals, shared about Rays of HOPE Ministries in churches and prayer meetings, without mentioning or asking for donations. Upon learning that Indian missions had a bad name around the Western world (because of their tendency to beg), he was grateful for listening to the Lord's prompting.

The first half of his Australian visit Manoj was hosted by Amanda and Darren, who went to the same Baptist church as Mike. The 60+ man, a CEO of a well-known Brisbane bank, invited Manoj to his office. Learning about Rays of HOPE Ministries, Mike was deeply touched. Since that time he and his wife have been faithful supporters of the Ministries with prayer and finances.

City Church was located near the bank where Mike worked. Knowing this congregation supported several India missions, Manoj requested a meeting with pastor Ben. When this pastor was in India the next month, they met again, this time in Mumbai. Manoj showed him around the different projects. (Two years later, in July 2012, a group of 18 Bible Students from Brisbane City Church came to Mumbai to volunteer in ASHALAYA and HOPE Center. The interns washed, cleaned, pained walls and cooked - a wonderful learning experience in servanthood for them, and a blessing for the staff and children.)

While in Australia,, Manoj mentioned to one of his hosts how wonderful it would be to one day visit Israel. The next day, when checking his email, he found Allison Nucciarone's letter about volunteering at ASHALAYA. As a result of the Nucciarones trip to Mumbai, Manoj received an invitation to be their guest in Israel and Jerusalem. (His dream was fulfilled in the beginning of 2012.)

The second half of the Australia trip Manoj stayed with Gary, whom he had translated many years ago while on a mission trip to India. Gary had been a great encouragement for the Ministries, but because of personal problems, his spiritual life had turned into a dessert. Sensing his friend's oppression, loneliness, hopelessness and anger, Manoj began to pray for the deeply wounded man. By God's grace, he was able to minister spiritually to Gary, who eventually agreed to come to a meeting with him. Manoj continued to pray for him, and thanked God when Gary later wrote him that he had returned to the Lord, and that He restored the years which the locust had eaten.

The spiritually fruitful trip to Australia was coming to an end. Two days before his return to Mumbai, a relation from his sister-in-law, living on a Church campus in a suburb of Brisbane, invited Manoj to a prayer meeting.
Arriving at the church, Manoj noticed the meeting already had begun. Between 40-45 people listened to a guest speaker from the USA. Manoj sat down on the last available chair in the back row. In the middle of his sermon, the preacher suddenly paused, pointed his finger at Manoj, and said, "I see a man from India. Please, don't

leave the building. I have to talk to you!"

After preaching, praying and ministering to the people, the American pastor (who didn't know Manoj) walked over to his Indian brother.

"I see that you are a church planter," he began. "The Lord has used you to plant several churches; God will use you to plant churches all over India and around the world."

"I see the Lord brought you to Australia for a specific purpose - ever since being here, you have never asked for money. The Lord shows me, that He will open the doors and windows of heaven, and pour such a blessing on your life and ministry that there shall not be room enough to contain it."

"I see the Lord opening doors of nations. He will take you to nations. You will not ask, but minister to Westerners."

"I see the Lord is about to release a huge piece of land for your ministry. On that land will be houses for orphans, widows and dying people, a hospital, printing press and bible school" (Manoj felt it was as if the preacher was reading from a brochure about the City of HOPE, without mentioning the name.)

That evening, Manoj returned home with Gary. He felt so blessed, fulfilled and excited, and so grateful that God had confirmed the vision and his calling for Rays of HOPE Ministries through this American preacher.

God honoured Manoj's obedience not to ask for money. Before he left for Mumbai, Amanda and Darren handed him the many anonymous donations for Rays of HOPE ministries they had received. Mike and his wife also blessed the ministry with a huge donation, while Sandy and Stephan, an elderly couple, adopted Manoj as their spiritual son. "We will be your prayer warriors for the ministry," they promised.

In 1992, part of the vision God had given young Manoj was that he would go to the nations and speak to many people. The Lord was beginning to open doors to other nations.

ASHALAYA'S PRECIOUS SONS ↑

AND DAUGHTERS ↓

THE IMPORTANCE OF
A GOOD SCHOOL

*E*ver since Manoj opened the orphanage, he desired to send the children to English speaking, private and well-known schools. The staff not only wanted to provide food, shelter and clothing, but also emphasise education. From experience Manoj knew that with an education, a child would be able to survive - it was an insurance for the future.

While growing up, Manoj attended the (low standard) municipal school in the slum where he lived. For ASHALAYA's children however, he wanted the best, which meant private schools which are very expensive. Even to register a child for a pre-primary school, parents have to pay a fee of $ 300. Added to that comes the $ 25 monthly tuition and bus fare.

Trusting God to open the way, Manoj filled in the application forms for ASHALAYA's children to be admitted to the school of his choice.

For no reason at all, his applications were rejected.

After a time of praying and fasting, Manoj filled in the applications a second time. While waiting for the answer, he prayed and believed God to make a way. The Lord answered their prayers - all children were admitted to the school.

Illustrative photo

But there was more: Rays of HOPE Ministries did not have to pay the registration fees, and received more than 50% reduction on the monthly tuition and bus fees.

Illustrative photo

The staff of Rays of HOPE Ministries noticed how the high quality of education effected their children - they saw a wholesome growth. Some of the children joined the school's sport team.

One daughter danced on stage before an audience of thousands of people. Her Ashalaya family was so proud of her!

At present, 90% of ASHALAYA's children are enrolled in English speaking private schools. The rest go to private Marathi-speaking schools. One such school, even though it is not categorized as Christian, is run by Christian management. For ASHALAYA this is a double blessing, as it enhances and strengthens what the children learn and experience at home.

India's new academic year always starts on June 13th. It is a time of heavy financial strain for the families. Each year, it is customary for a child to receive a new school uniform, sports clothing, a school bag, shoes, books, notebooks and pencils. This usually costs about Rs. 3,000 or $ 80 per child. Because the school doesn't supply anything, the items have to be bought from different shops.

In 2011, there were not enough funds to buy the necessary items ASHALAYA's children needed for the new school year.
The staff decided that their first priority was obtaining books and notebooks, so these were bought from the money that was available. They explained to the children why they had to go to school in their old uniforms, use their old school bags, and wear their old shoes. It was a difficult and painful experience, both for the staff and the

children - it was obvious to everyone they were wearing old uniforms, shoes and bags.

Manoj had been praying for the Lord to open doors and provide for the needs of the children. Help came from unexpected corners.
During the first school week, a few families approached him.
"We want to buy school uniforms for four or five children," they told Manoj.
Then he received a phone call from a non-Christian lady.
"Did you already buy schoolbags for the children?" she inquired.
"No madam, we are trying to raise funds to do so," Manoj honestly told her.
"How many children need schoolbags?" she wanted to know.
The next day, this woman informed Manoj that she had ordered schoolbags for all the children of ASHALAYA. "I already paid the company," she said. "The bags will be delivered within a week."

A Muslim family was used to celebrate their child's birthday at home in a lavish style. That year, they wanted to do something different.
"Why not celebrate our son's 5th birthday in an orphanage?" one of the parents suggested.
Not knowing where to go, they googled for a non-profit-organisation and orphanage in the Navi Mumbai area. "ASHALAYA - Rays of HOPE Ministries" appeared on their computer screen.
The couple made an appointment to visit Manoj in his office.
"We would like to celebrate our son's birthday with ASHA-

LAYA's children," they told him. "Would it be possible to visit the Home?"

Meeting the children deeply touched and impressed the Muslim couple.

"Yes, we want to celebrate the birthday here," they decided. "We also would like to buy a gift for each child. What do you need? What can we buy?"

"Well, to tell you the truth, our children need shoes for the new school year," Manoj told them.

"Can you give us a list with the name and size of each child?" the couple requested.

The next day, the family celebrated their son's 5th birthday in ASHALAYA. Instead of receiving presents, they blessed each child with a new pair of shoes. God provided, often in powerful ways, until every school need was met.

Outing with the children and staff of ASHALAYA

House church

Manoj's parents:
Tukaram and Muktabai

Tukaram   Muktabai

House Church

After the Sunday morning
meeting in a rented classroom in a Mumbai school

Manohar & Sangeeta

Some Staff Members and Helpers of Rays of HOPE Ministries

Manohar and Manoj had come to faith in Christ Jesus in the same period. Manoj went into full-time ministry and Manohar found a good job. From his income, he not only gave tithes to the church, but also supported Manoj financially. Manoj always hoped that his oldest brother too would go into full-time ministry. However, he knew he could not ask Manohar to make this sacrifice: give up his good salary and live a life of faith. Instead, he prayed for God to speak to his brother's heart.

In May 2009, **Manohar and his wife Sangeeta** told Manoj that the Lord had been speaking to their hearts - they were to join the staff of Rays of HOPE ministries as full time workers!

The couple took over many of Manoj's responsibilities and are now in charge of ASHALAYA's office and administration. This gives Manoj more time for the spiritual aspects of Rays of HOPE Ministries.

Always cooking for a crowd...

ASHALAYA HAS TO MOVE ~ AGAIN

*A*SHALAYA's premises were becoming overcrowded. 45 children, the caretaker couple, assisted by 6 widows and a few rescued sex workers (a total of 60 people) were now sharing the Home. The lease ended on January 15, 2012, and this time, the owner was not willing to extend the contract. However, because of the final exam periods, he graciously allowed them to stay in the house till the end of April 2012.

As the team prayed about the situation, the Lord spoke to their hearts: "It's about time you have your own place! Buy a house for ASHALAYA!"
It was a daunting prospect for a faith-based ministry. The estimated cost was around $ 450,000 (for a 225 sq meter ground plus three floors house) in Sector-12, Kharghar, Navi Mumbai (right in the present location).

Raising money to buy a house would take time. A lot of time. Which they didn't have. The 11 month contract was coming to an end. The family had to vacate the premises by April 30th.

> Since through God's mercy we have this ministry, we do not lose heart.
>
> 2 Corinthians 4:1

It seemed impossible to find a new Home for ASHALAYA. Manoj searched around, called agents, asked people, met with realtors, but everyone asked at least Rs. 35,000 (about $ 800) a month or more. Rays of HOPE Ministries could not afford such a high rent. The pressure of the looming deadline became heavier each day.

131

On April 20, Manoj received a phone call from a man who used to run a NGO home for children of labourers.

Four years previously, while Ashalaya was still using the 1-BHK flat, the couple had visited them. Because they received a lot of funding from overseas, the husband and wife thought about supporting both HOPE Centre and ASHALAYA.

However, after the visit, they decided to start their own home for needy children. Manoj didn't mind they had captured the concept. There was so much need, and now, more children could be helped and blessed.

The couple rented two big premises. Because there was no shortage of money, they installed air-conditioning, bought bunk beds for the children, and even hired personnel to help them for the children.

But after three years the husband and wife came to the conclusion that this kind of ministry was not for them.

"We have decided to close down the project," the man informed Manoj. "We will be vacating the rented premises. Are you perhaps in need of a place?"

Manoj could hardly contain his excitement. "Can I come over and see the building?" he asked.

The moment he saw the premises, Manoj knew their fervent prayers

> For whatever things were written before
> were written for our learning,
> that we through the patience
> and comfort of the Scriptures
> might have **HOPE**.
> Romans 15:4

were answered. The owner agreed to a rent of Rs. 20,000 ($ 400) a month.

Even though ASHALAYA's new home is the same size as the previous one, because of the way it is built, it feels more spacious. The couple even left a few bunk-beds behind! The new Home is located on a quiet side street, making it possible for the children to play outside and be safe. The previous building was on the main road, where traffic was heavy and dangerous.

The staff of Rays of HOPE Ministries continues to pray and believe that God will provide the funds to buy a building, which will serve as a permanent ASHALAYA home. Having to move a growing family every 11 months is too much.

That Sunday morning in church, Manoj preached about the different ways to dream.

"We can dream in the flesh, or have a dream that comes from God," he said. "One can dream of what he sees around him; or try to imitate, capture or attempt to be like someone else. Often, this behaviour is not successful. However, a dream from God is something He puts on your heart. This can either be a vision or a burden, but a dream from God NEVER gets lost, it is never wasted."

He mentioned the example of the couple who had everything going for them: thousands of dollars of support each month; use of cars and hired personnel. And in spite of all these material blessings, they had come to the conclusion it was not their calling to run a children's home.

The secret is being in the centre of God's will. Only then can you do His work, and continue doing so. People who are working out of their own strength, won't be able to do the work for long.

"We, at Rays of HOPE Ministries," Manoj continued, "have to

wait every day upon the Lord. We don't know from where our help will come , and how, but we pray and believe that it will come when we need it."

The staff continues to trust God to provide in supernatural ways. Often, help comes from seemingly impossible sources. Many times it is channelled through non-Christians who happen to pass by and visit ASHALAYA. God is at work! He is alive!

> I will lift up my eyes to the hills ~
> From whence comes my help?
> My help comes from the LORD,
> Who made heaven and earth.
> Psalm 121:1,2

Ashalaya family outing to Hill Station

A nutritious meal
to enjoy -
every day!

Cooked and served with love

Birthday celebration of an ASHALAYA child.
Everyone gets their own birthday cake!

FAITHFUL SUPPORTERS

Around the year 2000 Manoj first began to use the internet as a tool to evangelize. Via a Christian Chat room he met **LUKE** from Arizona, USA,. Luke was the only non-Indian guest at Manoj's wedding - a real attraction. Luke was also the very first International Mission Friend. He continues to be a faithful Rays of HOPE ministries supporter.

Another faithful friend is **Dr. Benjamin,** also from the USA. (See story page 97.)

Sunday evening church meeting with the Ashalaya family in a rented classroom

WEDDING JEWELLERY PROJECT

*I*n 2012, ASHALAYA no longer was called an orphanage, but a **family**. There were three 17 year-old daughters; one studied for her 12th grade exams. The other two girls, rescued from being sold into prostitution, had been too old for school. One girl received on the job training as a pre-primary teacher, while the other assisted the Home's caretaker team.

The first priority of Rays of HOPE Ministries is to give each child the best education possible. When that is not possible, they receive vocational training. One girl e.g. learns how to run a tailoring class. An educated child is empowered. The next step is to find Godly life partners for the daughters and get them settled.

In India it is customary for the family of the bride to provide a huge dowry and to buy gold ornaments as a wedding gift for the bride.

ASHALAYA cannot afford a dowry. Manoj and his staff trust the Lord to help them find men of dignity, who will accept the girls whole-heartedly and love them. They are to receive them as a blessing from the Lord, and not want them because of their money.

However, Manoj and Priya want to bless their ASHALAYA daughters with a wedding gift when the time comes for them to get married. This present consists of a pair of gold earrings, a ring and a necklace.

Illustrative photo

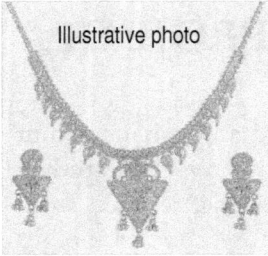
Illustrative photo

In 2011 they began saving Rs. 2,000 (about $ 50) each month. Hearing about a gold shop whose owner could be trusted, they deposited the savings with him. This non-Christian man eventually became a Mission Friend (see Chapter "How you can help") and has been supporting ASHALAYA in many ways.

In 2012, Manoj and Priya had enough savings to buy two pairs of earrings and rings for two prospective brides. This **wedding jewellery savings project** will be ongoing.

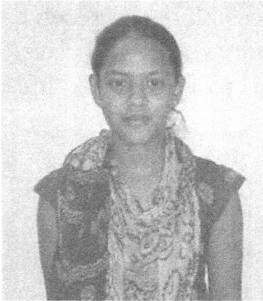

Two of
ASHALAYA'S
future brides

> At the end of our lives
> we will not be judged by how
> many diplomas we have received,
> how much money we have made
> or how many great things we have done.
> We will be judged by "I was
> hungry and you gave me to eat.
> I was naked and you clothed me.
> I was homeless and you took me in."
>
> Mother Theresa

TIME TO CELEBRATE!

$\mathcal{T}$he final school exams were over. The move to the new Home on May 2nd, 2012 was behind them. It was time to celebrate! The whole ASHALAYA family went for an overnight picnic on the other side of Mumbai, near the beach.

While there, Manoj received a phone call from a pastor friend living in the area, not far from another red light district.

"A CSW informed me about a fellow prostitute who died of AIDS," the pastor told Manoj. "Her two children, a 9 year-old son and ten year-old daughter have nowhere to go."

"I happen to be in the area," Manoj said.

"Can you come over?"

Manoj left the picnic and went to the pastor's house. After hearing about the plight of these children, Manoj agreed to meet them.

Seeing their need, Manoj didn't have to think long.

"They can come and live with us in ASHALAYA," he said.

"The boy has an infection on his leg," the pastor explained. "The woman who told me about these orphans promised to finish the treatment they already started at the local hospital."

He was to join Ashalaya a few days later.

Through Project ASHA, the team of Rays of HOPE Ministries ministered to a family of which both the father and mother were HIV positive. Recently, the father died of AIDS, and now the mother was in the last stage. The staff had often asked the parents if they wanted to place their children in ASHALAYA, but until now, the mother had been unable to part with her children - a 6 or 7 year old boy and a three year old daughter. Realizing she was to die of AIDS soon, the mother agreed for the children to move to ASHALAYA. Which brought the total to 47!

A NEW SCHOOL YEAR

At the beginning of May 2012, a group of Hindu ladies came together for a memorial service of a man whom they considered to be
a god. Even though the man had died in 2011, his birthday was celebrated throughout the region by his faithful followers.

"Why don't we celebrate our god's birthday in a unique way?"
one of the ladies suggested.

The idea found approval, but nobody knew what to do or how to
go about it. One of the women, who had been to ASHALAYA,
suggested, "Why not visit an orphanage and help them?"

She made an appointment with Manoj for the 4th of May and
shared the wishes of her friends.

"What can we bring?" she asked.
"Blankets? Or something else for the children?"

"Thank you, we have blankets enough,"
Manoj replied. "What we do need are items for
the new school year."

"What a fantastic idea!" the woman exclaimed. "How many children do you have?"

Each child received a new school bag.

Another group of Hindu ladies stopped by to
visit ASHALAYA. Touched and impressed by what they saw, they
too wanted to help.

"What do you need?" one of the women asked. "We want to
contribute."

"We are in need of schoolbooks for the children," Manoj replied.

When the new school year began, each child had everything it
needed. Again, God provided for the needs of the children.

140

A STORY OF HOPE
IN A HOPELESS SITUATION

Note: This is a true story, but in order to protect the identities of the people involved, all names are fictitious.

*I*t was during a prayer meeting in the slum church, that Devdas (Servant of God) met Prasiti (Ray, Hope) for the first time. He learned that the young widow had lost her husband about eight years previously. Poverty had made her desperate, and the only way the uneducated woman could earn some money was by prostitution. Selling her body to make a living, it was just a matter of time until she became HIV positive.

Despite her poor health, Prasiti became pregnant. Knowing that the slum community stigmatized a pregnant widow, she didn't know how to deal with the situation. What was worse, she also learned that her HIV had become AIDS.

I'm going to die, Prasiti knew.

Desperate to get rid of her unborn child, she attempted an abortion. When that didn't succeed, she tried to commit suicide. That too, failed.

A believer from the slum church came into contact with Prasiti. After sharing the Gospel with her, she invited the desperate woman to come to the prayer meeting.

Prasiti came, and gave her life to Christ. Believers prayed with and for her and counselled her.

"But what about my baby?" Prasiti wanted to know. "What will happen to the little one after I die?"

"Don't you worry," the staff worker of Rays of HOPE Ministries relieved her greatest fear. "Your child will be welcomed to

ASHALAYA, the House of HOPE. We will care for your baby, and love it for you. With all of our hearts."

But God had other plans for the unborn child.
Devdas, who had recently married, knew about the imminent birth of Prasiti's baby.

"Prasiti has given birth to a girl," the believer of the slum church informed him by phone. "But I have to tell you the mother is in critical condition, and has no money for medication."

"I'm on my way." Devdas immediately went over to the hospital. His heart went out to the bitterly crying baby, who obviously was in pain.

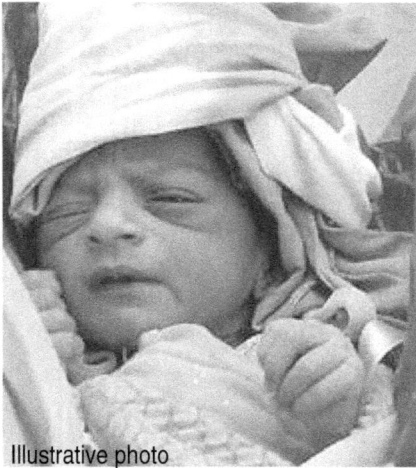
Illustrative photo

Taking the baby in his arms, to his surprise she immediately became quiet. Filled with compassion, he looked at the tiny face. *This little child is one of the thousands of children that Rays of HOPE Ministries is going to care for,* he thought.

Devdas began to pray for the little girl. "Lord God, I ask You to touch and bless this little one," he began. Then an amazing thing happened: it was as if a bolt of lightning went through this body.

This girl is to be part of your own family! God spoke to his heart.
Shocked to the core, Devdas couldn't accept it. Confused, he didn't know how to react. "Lord, if this is really from you," he softly prayed, "you better speak and confirm it with my wife!"

Looking forward to having their own children, Devdas didn't want to force a decision on his spouse.

"I'll be back," he told Prasiti. "I have to make a phone call."

From a quiet corner of the hospital and with a heart filled with trepidation, Devdas dialled Sara's number. His wife knew about the plan to take Prasiti's baby from the hospital to ASHALAYA. Sara listened to her husband conveying the story of the birth, and the plight of the mother. Devdas took a deep breath. "Sara, I have to ask you something very strange. Please, stop what you're doing right now, and start praying. Then get back to me and tell me what the Lord puts on your heart."

Ten minutes later his phone rang. Sara was crying, and could barely speak.

"You are not going to put the child in the orphanage," she finally managed to say.

"Why?" Devdas' heart was beating wildly.

"Because we are going to take her as our own baby, our daughter. We are adopting her into our own family," Sara whispered.

That afternoon, the couple visited the hospital to accept their God-given baby. Ashrita (protected by God) was born into their hearts.

"Do you think Prasiti wants to take her baby home?" Sara sounded anxious.

"Let's ask her," Devdas suggested.

"No, I'm already too weak to take care of her." The idea of bringing a newborn baby into the slum was too much for Prasiti. "I cannot breastfeed," she replied. "It will infect Ashrita with the HIV virus." She shook her head. "No, you take her home with you."

A few weeks later, Prasiti, the beloved daughter of the King, was welcomed into the waiting arms of her Saviour, Jesus Christ.

Devdas and Sara knew it was possible that Prasiti had infected her unborn child with the HIV virus. However, they had to wait 18 long months before Ashrita could be tested for HIV. That year and a half was a time of emotional highs and lows. The spiritual battle continued until the day of the blood test.

From the day she was born, Ashrita had been fed with powdered milk. She was not a healthy baby, and often sick. Each time the little girl fell ill, Devdas wondered if it was a sign of her being HIV positive. Then, the tentacles of fear clutched at his heart. The emotional struggle weighed him down.

Devdas and Sara wrestled in prayer over the life of their baby daughter. They reminded God of His promises in His Word, and spoke healing and life over Ashrita.

"Lord, we believe she is destined to live," Devdas said. "If she were meant to die, the abortion would have succeeded. God, you have brought her into this world, into our lives, not to be snatched away again. You have meant Ashrita for life, to be part of our lives." Each time the enemy tried to undermine their faith, Devdas and Sara fought the battle on their knees.

After another intense period of spiritual battle, the couple decided to take a bold step in faith. They were going to make a vow.

"God, we want to make a financial sacrifice," they promised. "We want healing for Ashrita. If the miracle takes place and she is HIV negative, then we will sow 1 *Lakh* into your Kingdom."

1 *Lakh* (about $ 2,000), was an enormous amount of money for a couple who were both in full-time ministry, and only received an allowance of Rs. 3,500 (about $ 70) a month. From this money, they had to pay their tithes, milk for the baby, food, rent and other family expenses. There wasn't much money left for savings, but the couple were willing to bring this painful sacrifice for their God-given daughter.

Months became weeks. Then days, and while the countdown began for the dreaded date, the couple continued to pray for a miracle. The life of their child was more important than anything else, even

more so than the financial sacrifice they had vowed to make.
For Devdas, the build-up of the emotional pressure became almost unbearable.

"I'm sorry, but I can't go with you to the pathology lab tomorrow," Devdas told Sara. "I can't handle the pressure. It's too much." Just to be away, he had scheduled another appointment.
On the day Ashrita was 18 months plus one day old, Sara took her to the pathology lab for the dreaded blood test.

"Call me, and let me know what's happening," Devdas told his wife.

"I'm at the doctor's office now," Sara phoned.
The female doctor knew the story of Ashrita. The woman had become a believer in Christ, and later a board member of RHM. To ensure that the identity of the baby would not be disclosed, the doctor sent Sara to a special laboratory.

"God is on our side," Devdas reminded his nervous wife. "He is with us. The Lord will answer our prayers!"
But even though his mind knew it to be true, his heart was bombarded with doubts and fear. The enemy continued to undermine his faith by whispering, *you're going to lose her!*

"I'm at the lab now," Sara updated her husband.
The people at the laboratory didn't understand why the mother was crying so much when they took the baby's blood for the test.

"It is done." Sara's voice trembled with emotion. "I'm going home now. They told me that we can pick up the lab results tomorrow."

"I don't have the courage to go there," Devdas admitted. "I'll call the doctor. Perhaps she can get the result even sooner than tomorrow."

Understanding their anxiety, the doctor promised to speak to the pathology lab, and call them the moment she received the test result.

Physically, Devdas was at the ministry meeting, but his heart and mind were elsewhere. He could only think of one thing: what's happening? With a heart filled with mixed emotions he picked up his ringing cell-phone and noticed his hand trembled. It was the doctor. His heart beating wildly in his chest, he asked, "What is it? A yes? Or a no?"

The doctor began to laugh. "Rejoice!" she said. "God has answered your prayers. Your daughter is HIV negative!"

Filled with wonder, Devdas and Sara looked at the printed test result they received from the pathology lab.

"God has been faithful to us," Devdas said. "Now it is time that we fulfil our vow to Him!"

Within a week, the couple sold their wedding jewellery and everything else they could find in order to reach their goal of Rs. 100,000. And as they had promised, this money was sown into the House of God.

In June 2012, Ashrita was old enough to go to school. Her proud parents stayed with her during that first three-hour school day. Devdas and Sara cannot imagine a life without her. Their God-given daughter continues to be a source of joy for them.

I am only one

but still I am one.

I cannot do everything

but still I can do something.

And because I cannot do everything

I will not refuse to do the something that I can do.

Edward Hale

A CITY OF HOPE
FOR THE HOPELESS

*T*hroughout the years, more and more projects have been added to Rays of HOPE Ministries. The vision to have a central place to house all the ministries was confirmed by many believers.

A prayerful search began for a suitable plot of land. Thirty kilometres from Mumbai, there were 30 acres of land that could be ideal for the building of the City of HOPE. Nearby roads make it possible to use the facilities of the big city.

Presently, the offices of Rays of HOPE Ministries and ASHALAYA are in Kharghar, Navi Mumbai, a district between Navi Mumbai and Puni city.

The staff and supporters of Rays of HOPE Ministries believe the Lord is going to prove His faithfulness. After all, He has done so throughout all these years. He is the same God, who is faithful and who will fulfil his promises.

Ever since Manoj shared his vision for the City of HOPE, local and worldwide supporters of the ministry have been praying and believing the Lord for land and resources.

We are looking forward to see how this work of God will become a reality.

Come, Let US Build...

A

City of HOPE

...a place of Refuge

Possible location for the City of HOPE

The path of life
leads upward
for the wise.

Proverbs 15:24

GOD'S LOVE IN ACTION

When the City of HOPE has become a reality, the majority of Ashalaya's children will move there. However, the staff realizes that it is also important to have a foothold in the city.

Over the last 3-4 years, ASHALAYA has received between 2,000 - 3,000 visitors. Most of them were non-Christian locals who heard about the Home, came for a visit, and kept coming back.

Over time, the staff saw that ASHALAYA not only cared for needy children, but at the same time was a blessing for non-Christians. The Home not only is a platform of indirect evangelism, it also serves as a local support base. The biggest part of ASHALAYA's living expenses are paid for by non-Christians. Therefore it is important to maintain this connection point, especially because the City of HOPE will be 20-30 km. away from the city. For many locals it would be too expensive to get there.

ASHALAYA connects people to the ministry and ministers to the visitors. In a non-threatening way, they are introduced to the love of Christ, and see God at work in the lives of the children and staff caring for them. Many visitors have shown interest in knowing more about Jesus. Being an example of God's love in action, the staff believes it is important to always have a small ASHALAYA family in the present location. (Or the building they hope to buy.)

Sympathy is no substitute for action.
David Livingstone, missionary to Africa

TIME LINE
Rays of HOPE Ministries

1979   Manoj born in Ghatkopar slum, Mumbai, India

1984   God heals Manoj from severe asthma

1991   Age 12, Manoj comes to faith in Christ Jesus

1992   Age 13, 1st vision from God that one day, Manoj would travel the world and speak to many people.

1994   Age 15, Manoj enters into full-time ministry

1995   Manoj's parents move out of Ghatkopar slum. Age 16 - receives the vision to establish ASHALAYA.

1997 - 1998   Residential missionology course - 1 year.

1999   Vision to establish Rays of HOPE Ministries

2000   Meets his future wife - Pinky

2001   Attends a Bible school in South India for 6 months.

2002   Rays of HOPE Ministries becomes an officially registered NGO - RHM

2005   2nd phase of Rays of HOPE ministry begins to unfold

2006   Opening ASHALAYA (House of HOPE) with 2 children

2007   October 15 - Opening HOPE Center in Thurbe, Red Light slum
             December 8 - Manoj and Priya (Pinky) marry

2008   Project Dignity is added to Rays of HOPE Ministries

2009   Vision for the City of HOPE is born
             ASHALAYA moves to bigger premises

2010   ASHA (Care Home) project begins with two children

2012   ASHALAYA moves again
             Rays of HOPE ministries celebrates its 10th anniversary

IN CLOSING

Writing the story about this humble Indian pastor, I have tried not to turn Manoj into a super hero, or a spiritual giant. He is not an angel, but a human being, with his strengths and weaknesses. He specifically asked me to mention that there have been occasions that he almost lost faith, or was tempted to give up. In those trying moments, God sometimes used a believer to lift him up; other times, Manoj received encouragement from God's Word, which helped him to get back on track, and revived his spirit.

Spiritual leaders are always prone to attacks from the enemy in the area of pride, money or moral conduct. Manoj is no exception.

God has protected Manoj from falling into sin, but there have been times that he literally had to run, like Joseph from Potiphar's wife.

Our brother and his family needs God's daily protection, grace, wisdom and help. He cannot carry the burden alone.

Manoj needs people who will bring him before the throne of grace, who are willing to pray for him on a daily basis. Only then will he be able to continue to do the work that the Lord has called him to: to make a difference in the lives of those who are without HOPE, and give them a future!

Are you willing to become a prayer partner?

Pastor Manoj Magar & Family

Rays of HOPE Ministries

MAN-PREET House, B22/2
Gharkul, Sector-15, Kharghar
Navi Mumbai-410210, MH, India

BECOME A RAY OF HOPE

The local body of believers in India, together with believers world-wide, can be an instrument to reach those who are lost in sin.
You too can make a difference in the lives of the hopeless and destitute in Mumbai by giving them a HOPE and a FUTURE.

Ways to help

1. **Sponsor an orphan child in ASHALAYA**
2. **Sponsor the CARE HOME**
3. **Sponsor the feeding program of HOPE CENTRE**
4. **Specific donations**
5. **Sponsor special occasions.** E.g. a birthday, anniversary, etc.
6. **Come in person and volunteer**
7. **Become a mission friend* to help build the City of HOPE.**

At least 1,000 partners are needed who are willing to commit themselves to pray and support the City of HOPE. 1,000 people willing to donate a minimum of $ 50 per month for the next five years (a total of 60 months), will enable the City of HOPE to become a reality.

* A Mission Friend can be an individual, a group of friends, a family, a Sunday School, a church or an institution, etc.

For I know the thoughts
that I think toward you,
says the LORD,
thoughts of peace
and not of evil,
to give you a FUTURE
and a HOPE.

JEREMIAH 29:11

www.ingramcontent.com/pod-product-compliance
Lightning Source LLC
LaVergne TN
LVHW051640080426
835511LV00016B/2403